Activities for Individual Learning through Shape and Colour

Also available from Continuum

100 Ideas for Teaching Creative Development, Wendy Bowkett and Stephen Bowkett

Let's All Play – Activities for Communication, Language and Literacy, Jenny Roe

Activities for Individual Learning through Rhyme, Wendy Bowkett and Christine Baillie

Activities for Individual Learning through Shape and Colour

Wendy Bowkett

with Christine Baillie

Resources available for download

Many of the worksheets are available online at:
http://education.bowkett.continuumbooks.com

Please visit the link and register with us to receive your password and access to these downloadable resources.

If you experience any problems accessing the resources, please contact Continuum at info@continuumbooks.com

continuum

To Christine, a special friend and valued colleague, and her family for giving us the time to make this book possible. Thanks especially to Lauren and Emma who made us giggle while suggesting alternatives to help the book along!

Wendy Bowkett

To Mum and Dad for all the love and support they've shown me throughout my life. Also to Iris and Ron for encouraging my love of books and drawing.

Christine Baillie

Continuum International Publishing Group

The Tower Building
11 York Road
London
SE1 7NX

80 Maiden Lane,
Suite 704
New York,
NY 10038

www.continuumbooks.com

© Wendy Bowkett with Christine Baillie, 2010

British Library Cataloguing-in-Publication Data
A catalogue record for this book is available from the British Library.

ISBN: 9781441155542 (paperback)

Library of Congress Cataloging-in-Publication Data
Bowkett, Wendy.
  Activities for individual learning through shape and colour / WendyBowkett and
  Christine Baillie.
    p. cm.
  ISBN 978-1-4411-5554-2 (pbk.)
1. Shapes–Study and Teaching (Early childhood)–Activity programs. 2. Colors–Study and Teaching (Early childhood)–Activity programs. I. Baillie, Christine. II. Title.
  QA461.B68 2010
  372.35'044–dc22
2009047748

Designed and typeset by Kenneth Burnley with Caroline Waldron
Printed and bound in Great Britain by Bell & Bain Ltd, Glasgow

Contents

About the book

This book, as its title suggests, is based on shape and colour. The activities can be explored by individual children or with groups, small or large. Some ideas may be familiar while others will be fresh and new. I hope you'll find all of them useful and exciting. The activities have been used in early years' settings where I have worked. Many were adapted or 'tweaked' as I went along so that any group of children of varying abilities, ages and needs could 'have a go'.

The title topics are divided into separate sections. These can stand alone or be used in a more integrated thematic way to suit the time you have available and the degree of detail you or each child wishes to explore. The modular nature of the sections means that each can form the basis of a 'mini theme' lasting a day, a week or longer. Each section covers all areas of the Early Years Foundation Stage.

Similarly, the activities within any section can be used separately and as self-contained units for individual or group learning. You will also find tips and suggestions for developing activities further if you want to, never forgetting that your ideas are very relevant too.

My intention has been to make this book as flexible as possible, with an emphasis on practicality. No expensive equipment will be required for any activity; most items will be found within or around your group's setting. However, having the use of a photocopier or scanner will save lots of time in drawing, copying or tracing the activity pages.

Some activities are set out like a recipe, with lists of the ingredients needed to begin and a method, with instructions, on how to start. With that metaphor in mind, the difference between the act and the art of cooking lies in your own creativity and willingness to try out new things. Once you have tried an activity as described in the book, consider how you might change it to make it more interesting and enjoyable for each child next time. Also give thought to mixing and matching activities from different sections to create new links and sequences.

Hopefully each early years' setting will have a wide variety of equipment and facilities, but each will differ. The ideas are deliberately not specific to a particular place. There is often little or no reason to stop you from providing any or many of the activities outdoors or in a park, for instance. If a table is needed for some games or art and craft activities, you may find that in your setting, these activities would also work just as well on the floor, with added protection for carpets or flooring.

The activity pages are designed in such a way that no child need fail – notice the difference between the following two questions.

How many triangles are in the picture?

How many triangles can you see in the picture?

One is set up for possible failure, while the other shifts the emphasis to become a matter of observation, and a skill that can be carefully developed.

If an idea seems familiar, familiarity does not need to breed contempt. It can remind us of splendid things we used to do and loved but that got buried along the way. It can refresh our thoughts and help us to remember other related activities too! How many times have you said, 'I can't remember the last time we did that?'

This book is intended to provide a resource of ideas and activities covering many aspects of the Early Years Foundation Stage. The activities are ideal for individual or group learning and are by no means the only way to do it. They worked for me in many different settings; hopefully they will work for you too.

For ease of reference I have used letters to denote the specific area, or areas, of the Early Years Foundation Stage that the activity relates to. These have been cross-referenced at the beginning of every section, so that you can see at a glance which activity relates to which area. As all the Early Years Foundation Stages are, in my opinion, of equal importance and should be encouraged and nurtured in any setting, I have listed them below in alphabetical order.

C – creative development
This area covers creativity, imagination and imaginative play, music and dance, exploring media and materials, and responding to experiences and communicating ideas.

CLL – communication, language and literacy
This area includes writing, reading, linking sounds and letters, talking, communication and listening skills.

KUW – knowledge and understanding of the world
A vast area of development that covers exploring and investigating, designing and making, time, place and community, cultures and beliefs as well as ICT skills.

P – physical development
This area covers the use of equipment and materials, movement, space, and awareness of body and health.

PSE – personal, social and emotional development
This area covers self-care, confidence and self-esteem, behaviour, relationships, attitudes and a sense of community.

PSRN – problem solving, reasoning and numeracy
This area of mathematical development covers numeracy, calculating and measuring, problem solving and reasoning, not forgetting shape and space.

Many activities are not specific to one area and will often overlap with others. We would have difficulty participating in most activities without some form of communication, copying patterns on a peg board involves more than mathematical skills, and playing board games requires more than an understanding of social skills. There are some activities which encompass all areas of development – one such example is cooking. So don't be put off by an activity with 'P' in the grid because you don't feel like moving about today (maybe fine motor skills are required) or avoid an activity with 'PSRN' in the box, mathematics is fun and doesn't always involve numbers.

So mix, match and enjoy!

Terminology

There are several terms used to simplify the text within the book.

When using the word 'child', I am mainly referring to children under the age of eight. If I refer to particular children, I have changed the names and very often the gender to protect their identity, but I use 'he' and 'she' randomly within the activities.

I use 'early years' practitioner' to describe any one of the many different people (volunteers and employees) involved in a setting with children under eight years old. This includes anyone working in a breakfast or after-school club, holiday play scheme, crèche, playgroup or pre-school, nursery or school, students, parents, childminders, nursery nurses, classroom assistants and teachers.

'Parent' is mentioned in the book to include anyone who lives with and takes care of a child on a day-to-day basis and is responsible for that child's welfare. They may be a grandparent, guardian or foster carer, to name just a few.

Why shapes?

There is shape and form in everything we look at and this was one of the reasons why shapes were chosen for the first part of this book.

Shapes can be free and easy like a doodling, or very strong and particular, as in classical Euclidian geometry. The latter are the ones I talk about in Part 1 of this book.

I have always enjoyed playing with shapes and doodling. However, my other colleagues have been less enthusiastic in 'doing' shapes as a theme because it's 'maths'. I want to show the fun you can have in developing mathematical understanding, both for adults working with children and the children themselves.

Most shapes are familiar, and little or no equipment is required to take advantage of the wealth of activities in each section. Templates are provided on pages throughout the sections so that they are on hand for immediate use.

You can find out more detailed information about any of the shapes mentioned here (and many others not included) by using an Internet search.

Why colour?

Colour is part of every day in a young child's life, beginning with recognising which toothbrush to use in the morning, to dressing in a favourite colour of T-shirt and does it match the trousers, as well as deciding which colour of cup to drink from and which ball to play with outside. One reason for choosing colour as one of the themes in this book is because most early years' groups use colour in matching and sorting activities and games. Usually there is a huge variety of equipment that is brightly coloured and therefore easy to incorporate into activities without time spent looking for relevant items. Colours are familiar to most people and little or no equipment is required to take advantage of the wealth of opportunities for using colour in every environment.

The shades and hues of colour everywhere we look will help children to improve their observational skills, while boosting their vocabulary and understanding of words and, in many circumstances, it will also increase their development in mathematics.

The first section involves activities that are not specific to one colour and can be used within other sections in Part 2. I have also incorporated some background information about each colour; a brief history of their significance in our lives and the meaning they hold for different people. Colours can evoke strong feelings and emotions which can give early years' practitioners the opportunity to enhance and extend children's imaginations and experiences.

You can find more detailed information about the symbolism and meaning of colours by using an Internet search

Safety awareness

Always be especially aware of health and safety issues when outdoors, as well as inside your setting.

Some activities may require safety mats or padded floors and would not be suitable for outdoor play unless your setting can provide adequate ground safety.

Always ensure that activities with small items are closely supervised and are kept out of reach of younger or less able children. Be aware of activities using items that are easy to put in ears or up noses. Children who still 'mouth' items need to be supervised on an individual basis to prevent swallowing of small objects, especially during craft activities.

Always use protective covers on bladed craft knives or similar, and after use place them well out of reach of the children *immediately*. It is such a temptation to carry on with the activity, leaving the knife within easy reach in case you require it again straight away. Even with 'one eye on it' and a protective cover on the blade, a craft knife is extremely dangerous to have anywhere near children.

Similarly, never leave children unattended with scissors. Even round-bladed children's scissors are potentially dangerous. Teach children to carry and pass scissors with their hand around the closed blades. If scissors are passed by the handles, the blades can easily open and cause injury.

Always wear protective clothing or aprons and gloves (if necessary) whenever paints, felt pens, dyes, glues and glitter, etc. are in use. Even washable paints can leave stains on clothing. Some of these items can cause allergic reactions in children and adults, so be aware of itchy skin or eyes and any type of swellings on hands and face.

Always ensure surfaces are protected or washable before using glue, paint or similar media and when involved in messy activities.

Tips and shortcuts

Activity pages can be adapted or altered for use with other ideas to suit individual children. If you need to use a more challenging game, puzzle or maze, just pick the most appropriate example from the book. Then superimpose other pictures on to your chosen page and you have a 'new' activity.

> **TIP** To erase a small image – take a photocopy of the specific activity page and use correction tape or fluid to block out the picture not required, then add the 'new' cut out image and photocopy.
>
> To erase a larger picture – before photocopying the activity page, cover the image not required with paper. After photocopying, add your new picture and re-photocopy.

Straight line cutting can often be achieved by children in early years' settings. However, whenever accurate cutting is required, i.e. when making games, it often means that early years' practitioners have to wield the scissors. On many occasions I've seen adults spending their lunchtimes or breaks cutting out shapes from sheets of paper. Very time consuming, especially if each image or sheet is the same.

> **TIP** When you need several examples of one shape or picture, staple a few sheets of paper together with the image you need on the top sheet and then cut it out. (While cutting 'one', you are producing several more.) Check the number of sheets of paper you can cut through neatly before stapling them together. A real time saver!

Some activities involve threading, and one pre-school I visited had beads and peg boards but no laces or blunt-eyed needles for threading. One practitioner had removed her shoe lace so that a child could 'sew'. I showed them how to make a lace, quickly and easily (see below). Shoes without laces can be very dangerous!

Place a piece of sticky tape (up to 10cm long) on a table, sticky side up. Choose your thread (which may depend on what is to be threaded) and hold it very firmly between your thumbs and index fingers. Stick it on to the tape near to one end. Fold this end of the tape over the thread and stick it in place, then roll this very firmly over itself until you have a stiff 'needle' for threading. Cut the thread to the length required and then cut the other end right up to the sticky tape. Your 'lace' is ready.

Often, when involved in a specific topic, particular types of equipment are needed on a regular basis. With shape and colour as themes, the requirements are obvious and, as early years' practitioners, we are always on the lookout for time-saving devices. Over a number of weeks, whenever there was a spare minute (usually the lull before the storm) we would add to our collage or shape boxes.

Initially we had a large cardboard box for collage materials, which included all manner of textures with fabric, buttons, wool, pine cones and papers of any description. However wonderful this box was to rummage through for the children, it soon became messy, tangled and difficult to spot the bit you really needed for your picture, especially if it was a small item right at the bottom of the box!

> **TIP**
>
> Collect plastic ice-cream containers. They stack well, can be labelled clearly, and are just the right size to contain enough different 'textures' to keep everyone happy. Get everyone involved, before long you will have more containers than you know what to do with, but it will keep these small bits and pieces tidier and easier to access.

Our shape box was full of a variety of cut-out shapes of coloured paper or card. It came about when, at the end of an activity, there were scrap pieces of paper left around. They were too big to cut up for our collage boxes and too small to return to the paper cupboard, so we would put them into a scrap paper box for use in other collage and craft activities.

> **TIP**
>
> Whenever you have a few minutes to spare, sit and cut out some shapes from these scraps of paper; don't forget to staple pieces together to save valuable time. Put them in a shape box which can be available for the children to use during many craft activities, particularly during shape themes.

I have a found a 'bits and bobs' box an invaluable tool wherever I worked. In spare moments, in between activities, while children were waiting to go outdoors, or as a general talking point, I would use one or two of the things from my box to start conversations, guessing games or songs. The box is only an eight centimetre cube but it can hold a variety of things. It always contained a string of ten different coloured beads, a folding ruler, a finger puppet, a tiny notebook and pencil and a surprise item.

> **TIP**
>
> If you haven't got a box – a pocket or purse will do!

Part 1: Shape

Section 1: Activities for all

	KUW	CLL	PSRN	C	P	PSE
1 All shapes and sizes	•	•	•			
2 Two dimensions		•	•	•	•	
3 Shape templates page	•				•	
4 Three dimensions	•	•	•			•
5 All wrapped up	•	•	•	•	•	•
6 Guess the gift activity page		•				
7 Unusual two dimensions		•	•	•	•	
8 Page of polygons		•				
9 Finding shapes	•	•	•	•		
10 Finding shapes activity page	•	•				
11 Shape dominoes	•	•	•	•	•	•
12 Shape dominoes game					•	
13 Tessellations		•	•	•	•	
14 Tessellations pattern page	•	•				
15 Progressive patterns		•	•	•	•	
16 Patterns of shape page	•					
17 Story telling		•	•	•		•
18 Symmetry	•	•	•	•		
19 Reflections activity page	•	•	•		•	

All shapes and sizes

I think it is very important when doing a topic like shape that early years' practitioners understand a little about geometry: the properties and attributes of shapes. I'm not suggesting that the children be taught all the technical details below, but adults working alongside the children should be aware of the differences between shapes and solids.

Geometry is a part of mathematics that deals specifically with questions of size, shape and position of figures in space. For simplicity, as we are working with under-eights in the main, there are two common subjects in geometry, plane and solid.

- *Plane geometry* is about flat shapes like lines, circles, triangles and rectangles; i.e. shapes that can be drawn on a piece of paper in two dimensions.

- *Solid geometry* is about three-dimensional objects like cubes, cylinders and pyramids. These three-dimensional solids are split into two groups. Polyhedras, with flat faces, include prisms and cuboids. Non-polyhedras include any solid with a non-flat surface such as spheres, cylinders, cones and rings (called torus).

I have often heard the wheel of a car being described as a circle. A wheel is in fact a three-dimensional object which has a surface (i.e. a two-dimensional face) which resembles the shape of a circle.

The top of a box may be rectangular in shape but the box is actually a cuboid.

A tube of Pringles® has a circular lid but the whole package is a cylinder.

Find other surfaces on three-dimensional objects that you can name as a plane shape while being aware of the solid's name too.

Obviously many pre-school children do not need to know these technical details, but it is vital, when teaching about shapes and solids, that the adults are aware of the differences.

Two dimensions

This activity involves matching pairs of shapes.

Ingredients
Two photocopies of the 'Shape templates page' (on card for durability), scissors and a closed box with an aperture cut in two opposing surfaces (each hole must be large enough for a child's hand to reach inside).

> **TIP**
> If you have shape templates available, allow each child to draw around a shape for cutting out. This is an ideal opportunity to develop hand–eye co-ordination and fine manipulative skills.

Method
1. Cut out the pairs of shapes from the photocopied card or use any shape templates you may have available.
2. Place one set of shapes in the box and place the other set on a flat surface so that they can be seen.
3. A child chooses a shape from those visible and places his or her hands into the box.

> **TIP**
> Often children find this task easier if they are given the opportunity to feel the shape before trying to find one the same in the box.

4. The child uses both hands to feel the shapes in the box and find the matching one. For younger or less able children:

   - Only use two shapes which are very different from each other, e.g. a circle and a triangle.
   - Add one shape at a time to the box once the child is familiar with the first two.
   - Cut each shape out of different textured card so that there is another attribute to 'feel' inside the box.

For older or more able children:

   - Vary the size of the shapes to be found in the box – have the larger shape on the table and a smaller one in the box or vice versa.
   - Use two pairs of different sizes of each shape.

A visiting student decided to complement this activity and made a drawstring feely bag which she had sewn with shapes all over the outside. She mentioned that the card shapes we used got very bent and creased, so she had cut some very colourful shapes from perspex. However, the edges and corners were so sharp that when you placed your hand inside the bag you could easily cut your fingers. She covered the edges with sticky tape and although that solved one problem, the shapes tended to stick together in the bag (possibly due to static friction) and were difficult to separate. She was very disappointed that her idea hadn't worked well but did use the shapes for a different matching game later on during her time with us.

Shape templates page

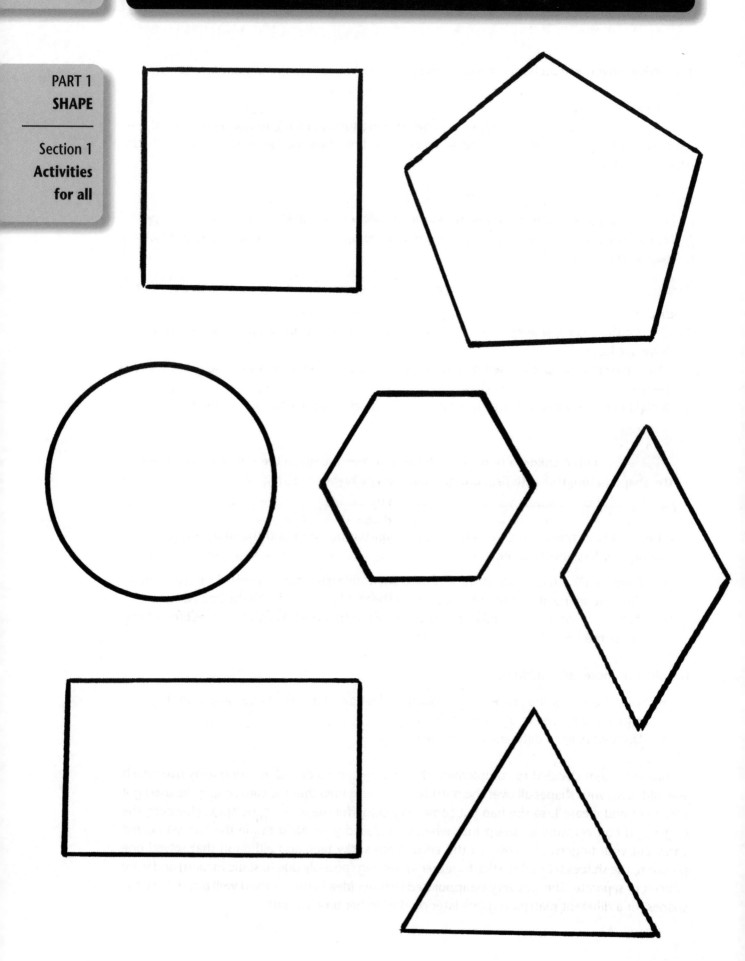

Three dimensions

The earlier activity for matching shapes can be extended to include three-dimensional objects. I found matching objects by touch much easier than the two-dimensional card shapes we used in the previous activity. The card shapes do tend to bend and crease and need replacing regularly, whereas the three-dimensional objects are solid and allow you to hold them firmly and really notice their shape.

Ingredients
A box with two apertures, a collection of pairs of matchboxes and bricks, beads, buttons and cotton reel 'inners'.

Method
1. Put one set of objects on a table or flat surface so that they can be seen and held, if necessary. Put the other set in the box.
2. The child chooses which solid they want to match up and puts hands inside the box.

> **TIP**
> Only place items that will fit inside the box with room to fully explore each one. If the items are too big, the child will not be able to use both hands in the box to find a matching solid.

> **TIP**
> Please try activities out yourself beforehand. The learning outcomes that you want for the children may not be provided by the idea you have created. For example, a team member could not understand how the children managed to complete her matching solid game so quickly, almost without having to 'feel' the objects in the box. It was only when a child mentioned that she had found the cold one that the member of staff tried the activity herself. The cardboard, plastic, wood, metal and foam solids all felt different because of their textures and warmth. Most of the children were matching those attributes rather than the shape of the items. Sorting by warmth would be a good activity too, though!

Often, when one idea generates a different learning outcome, it can be an advantage and may lead to other things. Observing, listening and understanding how each child involves himself in a game will help in your record-keeping as long as you are aware of the objectives of your activity. If you want children to notice differences in the shape and not the texture of the surfaces of the solids, then provide appropriate items in the box and always 'test' them out yourself.

For a much simplified game, use small-world toys in the box for the children to match. Try with metal or plastic objects like toys cars, buses, trains, aeroplanes and lorries, or beads, buttons, cotton reels and cubes.

For more able children, use different sizes of solids to match.

All wrapped up

Christine and I devised the 'Guess the gift activity page' after we had wrapped some objects for a guessing game. It was one of the funniest and most frustrating activities that I have ever done with a group of children.

The activity came about accidentally and was not planned at all. I was quietly wrapping some objects to play a 'Guess the gift' game when a couple of children came over to see what I was doing. They thought we were going to play pass the parcel and wondered whose birthday it was. When I explained that the presents were for a game, they asked to help.

I gave them some recycled wrapping paper, cut strips of sticky tape (which I attached to the table edge) and a toy double-decker bus. The paper was already cut to size for wrapping the bus. They started well, rolling the paper over the bus and sticking the overlapping edges together. The fun started when the sticky tape got caught, the paper became torn and the bus dropped out of the parcel. Trying to fit the bus back into the half-done wrapping crumpled the paper. The frustration but fun grew as the paper tore again and more tape was applied. Suffice to say the finished wrapped gift looked like a piece of patchwork having been pulled through a hedge backwards. However, the children enjoyed the experience and it led on to other activities involving estimating and measuring, cutting and sticking, co-operation and making decisions, covering many of the early years' foundation stages.

> **TIP**
>
> I have since realised that masking tape is easier than sticky tape for young children to use. It can be torn quite easily, no scissors are required and, if it sticks to itself, it can usually be pulled apart. It can also be painted or crayoned on to add to the effect.

A group had fun timing each other (by counting as well as using a stopwatch) to see how long it took to wrap a plastic car. Was it easier and quicker to wrap a teddy bear or book?

Try wrapping objects to disguise their appearance. How do you wrap a ball so that it doesn't look like one?

> **TIP**
>
> Collect wrapping paper from cut flowers, presents or paper bags. The paper we used had been used at least once beforehand and was given from parents, etc. When the activity was over we salvaged what we could to put in our collage boxes. (See 'Tips and shortcuts').

Why not give wrapping a go!

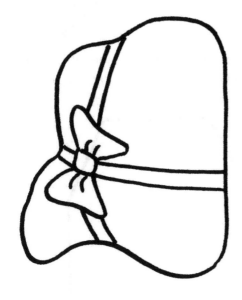

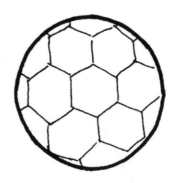

Polygons are two-dimensional shapes, made of straight lines, never curved. The shape is always closed, i.e. the lines are all connected with no gaps.

A simple polygon has only one boundary and never crosses over itself, e.g. a rectangle, triangle or hexagon, whereas the straight lines in a complex polygon intersect, making two or more shapes.

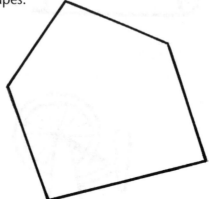 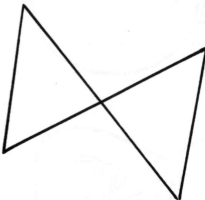

A convex polygon has no angles pointing inwards, i.e. angles that are more than 180°.

However, a concave polygon will have at least one internal angle greater than 180°.

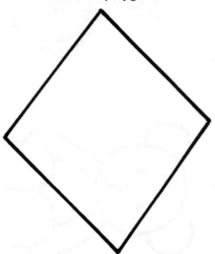 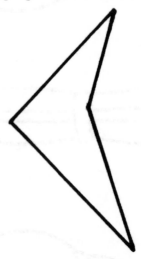

If all the angles in the shape are equal, and all the sides the same length, then it is a regular polygon, e.g. a square or equilateral triangle. Unequal angles and lengths of different sizes make the polygon irregular.

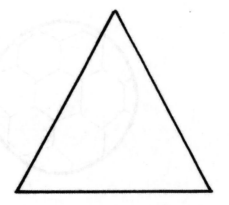 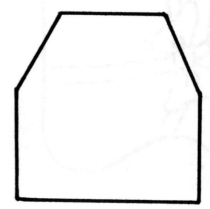

Although this may seem quite technical, I have watched children doodling; making straight lines that twist and turn over each other and join up at the starting point again. Until recently, I was unaware that most of these drawings had a name, i.e. complex polygons.

However, if you have ever watched a child when she first draws a triangle, you will be aware that drawing straight lines that join up as a shape is not an easy task for a young child to do.

Understanding this sparked off the next activity, making polygons with strips of card.

Ingredients
Strips of card of varying lengths but of the same width, hole punch and split pins.

Method
1. Punch holes in both ends of each strip of card.
2. Start with four strips of card of different lengths.
3. Join each end of each strip together with a split pin, making a long strip. Then join the two ends together to make a four-sided shape.
4. Move the sides around to form different shapes. Try a simple or complex polygon, or one that is concave or convex.
5. Use the shape made for a stencil or template to make patterns on paper.

> **TIP**
> Add sticky tape to the back of the split pins to prevent the strips from moving out of shape when drawing around them. Place white-tac on the back of each strip to stop the shape from slipping.

There are many ways of extending this activity. Below are a couple of examples which may encourage you to experiment with other ideas.

- Add extra strips as more unusual shapes can be made with five, six or more sides.
- Use two different lengths of card and join them together alternately to see the shapes that can be made. How do the shapes change if the strips are then joined together in a different way?
- Try making letter shapes with the joined-up strips.
- What happens if you use strips that are all the same length?

> **TIP**
> The 'Page of polygons' has several examples which can be copied to give a child a starting point.

Older children, or children with good hand–eye co-ordination, may enjoy making shapes with a ruler and pencil. Begin by drawing a straight line along the ruler edge. Then, without removing the pencil from the paper, swivel the ruler around the pencil tip and draw another straight line along the ruler. Continue in this way until you decide to join the lines at the start. No two shapes will be the same. Try it and see!

Page of polygons

Finding shapes

The 'Finding shapes activity page' means what it says. It is an active search as not all the shapes to be found match the examples exactly. There are regular shapes, i.e. each shape has internal angles of the same size and sides of the same length, and irregular shapes; the sizes also vary.

When a couple of children tried this activity, each decided on a different way to record the shapes they found.

Christopher loved numbers and could write numerals, so he decided that each shape he came across would have numbers written in them. His choice of numbers puzzled his mum when she collected him later. He had used one, three and four. Why? The circles he found were number one because they only have one line, triangles had number three written inside them because they have three sides, and the squares were number four. He had also recorded the total number of each shape in the example at the top of the page.

Sophie coloured each different shape with felt pens. The colours of the overlapping shapes were a little confusing for counting totals but the effect was very colourful.

Try using the three primary colours for the three shapes to see what the effects would be.

One of the pre-schools where I worked had a selection of Invicta Plastics Ltd shape templates which the children used to make their own jumble of shapes page, although the same idea can be achieved by using the shapes cut out onto card from the 'Shape templates page'. Then all that is required for a jumbled shape page is a piece of paper, a pencil, a little imagination and patience and a steady hand.

> **TIP**
>
> To prevent the shape templates from slipping when being drawn around, put a small blob of white-tac on the reverse of the shape to be used and stick it to the paper.

The activity can be extended by looking for shapes within your setting. We had found many items with circular and rectangular surfaces and were astounded when a little two-year-old suddenly shouted that the cow she was playing with in the farmyard had circular eyes but not circle spots! Once the children had been made aware of this, they looked more carefully and noticed the rectangles of the bricks on the farm buildings, the circular shapes on top of Lego® bricks and even the heads of drawing-pins on the notice boards.

Use trips to the shops or park to encourage these observational skills further. Picture books, catalogues and magazines are excellent alternatives to looking for shapes around and about.

Finding shapes activity page

Shape dominoes

The shape dominoes game is played in exactly the same way as ordinary dominoes except that instead of dots representing numerals, there are six different shapes to match. Photocopy the 'Shape dominoes game' page onto card and then cut out each domino before starting the game.

There are numerous ways to use the same page for other activities or to make other games.

Communication, language and literacy can be developed with the auditory and observational skills, concentration and memory required for the following game.

1. Place all the dominoes face upwards.
2. Ask a child to pick out a card with two shapes on it, e.g. a circle and a square.
3. If playing in a group, the child then asks his or her 'neighbour' to find a card with a rectangle and a circle on it, for example. Play continues in this manner until all the cards have been collected by the children.

If playing with an individual child, you may only want them to find four or five examples before ending the game. Your judgement will depend on the child's level of concentration, interest and ability.

> **TIP**
> Limit the number of cards and shapes to correspond to the children's level of development. If a child only recognises two shapes, only introduce a new shape one at a time.

Personal, social and emotional development should be encouraged by playing any game in a group. Joining in, taking turns, waiting patiently and working co-operatively with others are fundamental skills required when playing games.

Knowledge and understanding of the world will be enhanced by giving children the opportunity to make decisions and join in discussions about which colours to use for each shape on the cards. Then they can ask each other to pick out a card that has a blue circle and a purple hexagon on it, for instance.

Cut each domino in half to promote hand–eye co-ordination and fine motor skills while, at the same time, make a new game of snap, pairs or happy families.

> **TIP**
> You may need to discard several cards of each shape for happy families to work well. The game is usually played with four cards of the same motif (not eight, as is available on the dominoes page). However, with older and more capable children it works extremely well if the shapes are coloured in two different colours. Then you have an added attribute to work with during the game, enhancing problem-solving and mathematical skills in abundance.

Discussing the number of sides of shapes and using them for sequencing can boost a child's mathematical development in matching, numeracy and pattern making.

Shape dominoes game

⬜	⬜	⬜	⭕
⬜	△	⭕	⭕
⬜	⬡	⭕	⬡
⬜	▭	⭕	▭
⬜		⭕	
⬜	⬠	⭕	⬠
△	△	⭕	△
△	⬡	⬡	⬡
△	⬠	⬡	▭
△	▭	⬡	⬠
△		⬡	
⬠	⬠	▭	▭
⬠	▭	▭	
⬠			

Tessellations

PART 1
SHAPE

———

Section 1
Activities
for all

There are some wonderful colouring books on the market – with no pictures. Each page is a mass of lines and shapes that make elaborate patterns. Many are formed from basic tessellated shapes.

A tessellation is a collection of plane shapes that fill an area with no gaps and no overlapping, and are used for patterns and patchwork quilts. Mosaics and tiling are probably the first forms of tessellation using only small squares in chequered or simple patterns.

Interlocking jigsaw puzzles are also tessellations, sometimes with irregular shaped pieces too. In fact, any design using birds, animals or vehicles that fill a page without overlapping and no gaps, is a tessellation. M. C. Escher did some brilliant tessellated artwork.

Triangles, squares and hexagons are the only regular shapes which tessellate by themselves without additional shapes added. Any polygon with more than six sides, however, will overlap and need other shapes added so that they can tessellate.

Pentagons will tessellate without the need for another shape, but the pentagon will not be a regular one.

The examples on the 'Tessellations pattern page' will give you some idea of the many different patterns that can be created. Give your children the opportunity to make their own mosaics and patterns by providing them with squares, equilateral triangles and regular hexagons already cut out of paper or card. Ensure there are triangles, squares and hexagons where the sides are the same length so that different shapes will fit together easily. Use coloured paper to create varied effects in the patterns. They can be used within a colour theme too!

> **TIP** Refer to the 'Tips and shortcuts' section of this book (p. xv) for information on cutting several shapes out at the same time to save you time.

An alternative way to tessellate from cutting out shapes and sticking is to print shapes with paint.

Printing tessellations

Ingredients
Foam, scissors (or craft knife), shape templates, corks (or dowelling pieces), glue, paint, brushes and paper.

Method
1. Cut shapes from the foam using the templates and scissors – make two or three of each shape.
2. Glue each shape to a cork and leave to dry.
3. Brush paint over the surface of a shape and print it onto paper.
4. Repeat with the same or a different colour, placing this painted shape against one side of the previously printed one.
5. Continue in this way until the sheet of paper is full or the pattern is complete.

Tessellations pattern page

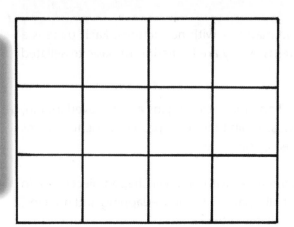

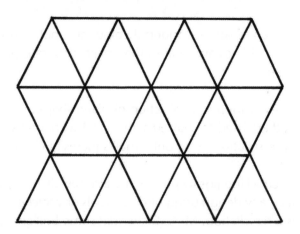

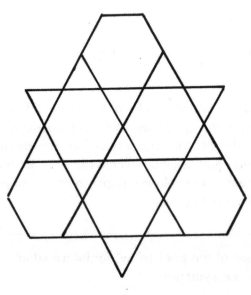

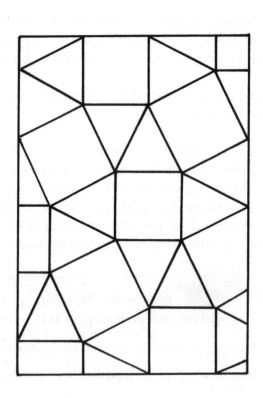

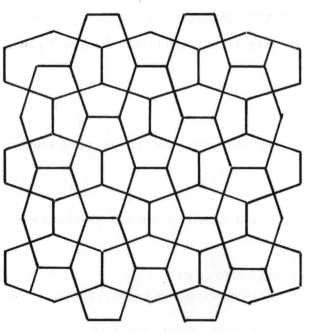

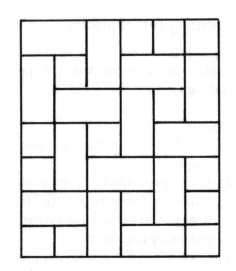

Progressive patterns

Inspiration for the following activity came to me when I had spent some time cutting out a handful of small squares, triangles and circles for an idea I was going to try that afternoon. I had carefully placed the shapes, in separate piles, on a piece of card. As I was walking across the room to put them on top of a cupboard, a child accidentally knocked into my arm and most of the shapes fell to the carpet. They fell haphazardly and, as we bent to pick them up, I noticed how some of them had fallen in patterns. Four squares had landed side by side in an almost square shape. Two circles were next to two triangles with another circle next to two more triangles, almost a perfect pattern or sequence.

I mention in Part 2: 'The sunny flower game' activity, how much I enjoy colouring in. Perhaps I have a streak of compulsive behaviour because I also love sequencing and patterns, placing things in order. As I picked up the shapes, I started to name them, one circle, two triangles, one circle, two triangles, etc. A couple of children joined in, making their own sequences and another idea was born!

The 'Patterns of shape' page I arranged so that the difficulty increases the further down the page you go. Some of the sequences may be too complex for the younger children in your setting and so the page is designed so that each pattern can be used separately.

Photocopy the page onto card and cut out each 'line'. The empty boxes at the ends of the patterns should be filled with the appropriate shape to complete the sequence. There are a few ways this can be done, depending on the age and ability of each child.

For older children or those with well-developed fine motor skills:

- The individual shapes can be drawn in the empty boxes.
- Place objects which have a surface the same shape as required, e.g. buttons, in the empty spaces.
- Photocopy the page again and cut out each box with a shape in it. These smaller cards can be placed in the empty spaces to carry on the patterns.

Younger children often find the option of handling the shapes while naming them in sequence an easier task. Giving children a visual and auditory clue helps their thought processes, while handling adds the kinaesthetic dimension to their learning.

Experiment with these and other ideas to observe the differences in individual children's thinking and developing skills.

Patterns of shape page

Story telling

The shapes I mentioned in 'Progressive patterns' were intended for use in the following activities. When we were spotting shapes in and around the nursery, I realised how easy it would be to convert those three-dimensional objects into two-dimensional ones.

With the cut-out shapes spread over a table, and paper and glue sticks on hand, I showed the children how the house across the road would look transferred to paper – a square with a triangle on top. It was very simple but conveyed exactly what I had been looking at. 'But what about the windows and door?' asked Chloe. 'Are you going to make the tree as well?' I suggested that each of the children make a picture with the shapes for us to guess what it was.

Immediately there were numerous houses like mine and some had windows, one looked like a block of flats with so many windows there were no walls. There was a tree with circular apples growing on it, lollipops, ice creams in a cone and even a meal of peas, carrots and rectangular sausages.

Good use was made of the circles with caterpillars, faces and flowers of all different colours. One picture had shapes dotted here, there and everywhere. When I said that I didn't think I had ever been where her picture was, Sophie said, 'Of course you have. It's the park! That's the trees, here's the slide, there's the red roundabout and these are the swings and they're very difficult to make you know.'

During story time that afternoon, we collected the Fuzzy Felt® box and began to put shapes on the story board. We used Sophie's idea of the park and roundabout, except it was green because the red felt circle wasn't big enough to be the roundabout. Felt children made from circles, triangles and rectangles enhanced our wonderful story about a (rectangular) dog who could talk and was in charge of the park.

Following on from that activity we cut more shapes from felt to add to the box because the popularity of making up stories from simple shapes grew.

It also led on to a shape display of a twelve-foot-long train running along the skirting board in the corridor. It was comprised of many sizes of rectangle, a couple of semi-circles, a square or two and circular wheels. The children made self-portraits from the shapes and each one peeped from the windows of the carriages. It was much admired by the children, who loved the fact that they were on a train going to the seaside while still at nursery! Yet another one of our stories.

Symmetry

When you fold any shape in half, and one half exactly covers the other, then that shape is symmetrical. The fold is the line (or axis) of symmetry. If you place a mirror on that line of symmetry then the shape reflected in the mirror will look exactly the same as the original image. The line of symmetry is sometimes called the mirror line.

The mirror needs to be frameless for the activity to work well so that the edge lies on the line of symmetry enabling you to see an unbroken reflection. If you do not have access to a mirror without a frame, then try silver card. Some types give a clear reflection; or fold aluminium foil over a thick piece of card, ensuring there are no crumples or ridges. Alternatively, fold the paper shapes to find the lines of symmetry.

Some shapes have more than one line of symmetry, and many are not symmetrical at all. The 'Reflections activity page' has many examples. Try folding each shape in different ways to find 'new' lines of symmetry, e.g. from corner to corner, across the widest or longest part.

Photocopy the 'Reflections activity page' and decide which shapes have lines of symmetry and then try some of the images on other activity pages.

Does a parallelogram have any lines of symmetry? A rectangle may look as though it has more than two – one across its width, another along its length, but how about its diagonal? If you fold it from corner to corner will you discover that the halves exactly cover each other or not? What happens when you try with a square? Fold a circle and see how many lines of symmetry you discover!

Are the kite, flower head and heart symmetrical? Look very carefully at the mirror images and the actual picture. Always check any lines of symmetry that you find by folding the image to see if both sides match exactly.

Extend the activity by including simple three-dimensional objects to see if two halves match. We were playing in the sand tray when a child brought a mirror to us to see if a bucket and spade had lines of symmetry. The children discovered that if the handle of the bucket was positioned carefully, then the bucket was indeed symmetrical. Most of the sand toys and even the shapes the moulds made with wet sand were examined and found to be symmetrical. The mirror did get a little scratched with the grains of sand but it turned out to be a very interesting half an hour or so.

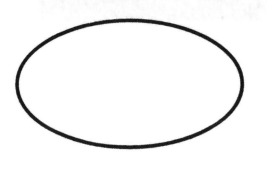
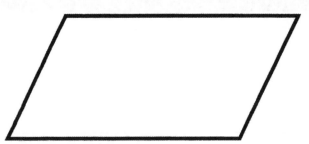
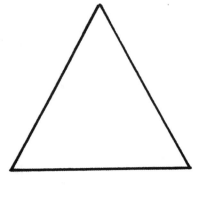

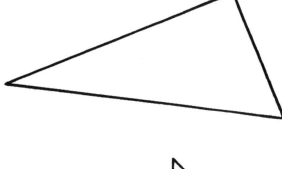

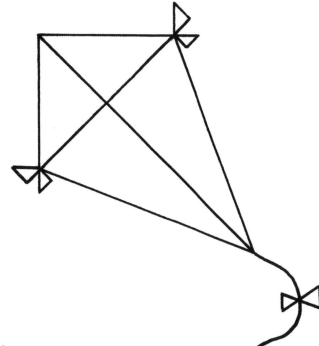

Section 2: Circle

	KUW	CLL	PSRN	C	P	PSE
20 What's special about being a circle?	•		•		•	•
21 Circular snacks	•	•		•		•
22 Circular pictures		•		•	•	•
23 Circle pictures page		•				
24 Circular games		•		•	•	•
25 Stepping stones		•			•	•
26 Semi-circle activity page	•					
27 Semi-circle fun	•		•	•	•	
28 Snap differences	•	•		•		•
29 Snap differences game page		•			•	

A circle is one of the simplest shapes in geometry. It is actually an oval (or ellipse) with a difference; which is to say, a special case of the category ellipse. Both shapes are made from one continuous line that joins up.

An ellipse is often thought of as a squashed circle and has two centres of focus (called foci). If you start at 'A' and go to any point on the ellipse and then go to 'B', add the two measurements, the distance will always be the same.

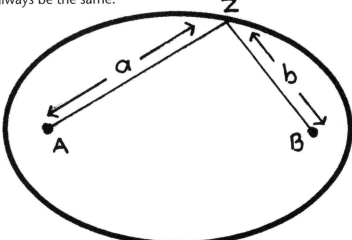

A circle is a special ellipse because both the foci are in the same place, at the centre. If you start at the centre and go to any point on the circle, the distance will always be the same and is called the radius. Any line of symmetry passing through the centre of a circle is called a diameter, and the distance around a circle is the circumference.

Many early years' settings have a circle time. Why is it called that? Do the children actually sit in a circle? What is the circle used for? Would chairs or mats in rows work better?

Our circle time included whoever wanted to join in. It was for reflection, to discuss the activities of the day, new ideas or occurrences, to share personal feelings about significant things, attitudes and behaviour or even future planning. The member of staff would invariably sit on a mat at the children's level and everyone was actively encouraged to express opinions and ideas. It was understood that any comments would be respected, listening to others is important and vital, and each person had the opportunity to join in if they wish.

Circle time can help children communicate more easily because it promotes a sense of belonging and security where they can safely express their feelings and make choices. It can also boost a child's self-esteem to know that their opinions are encouraged, listened to and respected. These times should be enjoyable for children, always ensuring there is a positive focus to the discussion.

If you have circle time to keep everyone in one place at the end of a session to enable staff to tidy up before children are collected, then perhaps you need to rethink or rename this particular time of day.

King Arthur had a round table where he and his knights would meet and sit. There was no head to the table, suggesting to all that each knight was of equal value to the king. How wonderful to feel as one with your head!

Circular snacks

During this circle-themed week, we decided to have circle snacks: only items that were shapes like circles could be eaten.

Our snacks were usually very healthy, comprising fruit, cheese or savoury crackers, and initially we had round crackers, muffins and crumpets, sliced bananas and grapes; nothing really different from an ordinary day.

Then, instead of having wedges of apple and oranges, our cook suggested slicing the fruit from top to bottom to make apple rings and orange slices, just like she did when making flans or pies. Oranges had never been so popular! I think they were much easier to handle and eat. The children became very aware of how the shape of something changed when sliced, and we experimented with cross-sections of all sorts of fruit. The children began to realise that fruit and vegetables have to be roughly cylindrical or spherical in shape to make a circle slice. Carrots and cucumbers worked well, as did peaches and nectarines, but celery didn't give us the right shape at all!

We used a small circular pastry cutter (used for making decorations on the top of pies, etc.) to make circular pieces of cheese.

As parents were drawn into the idea of circular snacks by their children, and knowing that we ate healthy foods, they asked if sweet biscuits could be brought into nursery for a change. It was amazing to see the variety of sweet biscuits that are round. Jammie dodgers and choc-chip cookies were the favourites, with rich tea and digestives coming way down in the long list of round biscuits.

A parent also brought in a few packets of hoop-shaped crisps which the children loved to place on their fingers before eating. We ate Cheerios® in a similar fashion and, when asked about other cereals, we did find that if you carefully cut a rice krispie in half across its width, it has a circular cross-section. This wasn't easy to do and needs a steady and delicate hand.

Mini pizzas

Ingredients
Slices of bread, pastry cutter, tomato purée, grated cheese, slices of Peperami®, oven or grill.

Method
1. Cut the bread with the pastry cutter into circles and toast one side.
2. Allow the toast to cool.
3. On the untoasted side spread tomato purée and sprinkle some grated cheese over the top.
4. Add a slice of Peperami®, if liked, and grill for a couple of minutes, or until the cheese melts.

We couldn't please one little girl who liked sliced olives on her pizza, and they're round too!

Circular pictures

I really enjoy giving children the opportunity to try things out, with no right or wrong outcomes. When we had circles as a topic, we found numerous examples around our setting; through the windows, in the playground and on walks.

We had already tried converting the three-dimensional solids we saw into two-dimensional shapes (see 'Story telling' in Section 1: Activities for all) and wondered how easy it would be to make pictures from just circles.

When children begin to draw pictures, a person is often one of the first images they produce, usually depicted as a round shape with eyes and a mouth. So we started this activity by giving each child just one circle each to make into something else. By adding a few lines to this circle we made faces and people, balloons, cherries, biscuits and pizza.

> **TIP**   To save time cutting out paper circles, use pre-cut tissue paper circles instead. They are cheap and easy to use, stick well and are available from most educational suppliers.

Then the children were given two circles of different sizes. A couple of rabbits, a cat and a variety of birds were made, with drawn lines for ears, legs, beaks and whiskers.

Even though it was the middle of summer, one young man made a snowman, where he had cut another of the circles into a rectangle for his hat!

We left a variety of circles of different colours and sizes for the children to carry on making pictures, some children made spotty pictures, like a dotty collage and very effective when displayed together on a notice board. One little girl used only brown and white circles on her paper. It was her Dalmatian which had brown spots instead of the usual black.

Ben, who loved grapes, made a bunch of them, although they were multicoloured as he couldn't find enough green circles because someone else had used some to make a caterpillar.

Samantha crayoned a huge area of blue across her sheet of paper and stuck circles on top. At first she said they were clouds in the sky, then she mentioned to her friend that they were really stepping stones for crossing the stream at the bottom of her garden.

Samantha's aside to her friend led me to think up a game to play in the garden later.

The 'Circle pictures page' gives a few examples, but there are many more images that can be designed with just circles in mind.

Circle pictures page

Fabric circle play

If you are unable to borrow a parachute from your local toy library or another pre-school setting, any light fabric cut into a circle will be as good to use as a purpose-made parachute. The circumference of the fabric will determine how many children can participate in the activity as each child needs to hold the edge of the fabric with both hands.

When using a parachute for the first time, explain that everyone must work together and not let go of the edge until it is their turn to go underneath. Plenty of space is required for parachute play and if you decide to use it outdoors, remember that a sudden gust of wind or slight breeze may pull the fabric from the children's grasp.

Start by laying the fabric down and position the children kneeling around its edge. Show the children your thumbs which tuck under the fabric with the rest of your fingers on top, in the 'parachute grip'.

Count to three and everyone stands up, still holding the fabric, and then extends their arms upwards, without letting go. The fabric will rise and then slowly drift down again. This action can be repeated as often as required, building up the duration of the activity as the children's arm and shoulder muscles will tire quite quickly.

> **TIP**
> Adults should make sure they do not extend their arms fully, as the action will pull the fabric from the children's hands next to you.

Try smaller circles of fabric with three or four children holding the edges so that they can discover the type of movements they need to make with their arms to make the fabric billow and float. (See further ideas in *100 Ideas for Teaching Creative Development* by Wendy and Stephen Bowkett, Continuum, 2008.)

Bang a drum

We had great fun with our marching band (*Activities for Individual Learning through Rhyme* by Wendy Bowkett and Christine Baillie, Continuum, 2010), and during our circle week, what could be more appropriate than only using circular instruments to march along with?

Our drum and tambours were very popular, beating a steady rhythm as children marched up and down the corridors. We also had cheerleaders with circular pom poms attached to their wrists, although the drum beat too slowly for some reason!

After the children had found castanets, finger cymbals, tambourines and coconut shells in our music trolley, they made a band. With chairs in a circle for a bandstand, like the local park, the children set to. I wouldn't have paid to listen, but a good time was had by all!

Stepping stones

Samantha's picture (in 'Circular pictures') brought this idea of a game to life: to get from one side of the stream to the other using stepping stones.

Ingredients
Card circles at least 20 centimetres in diameter (to fit a child's feet), a dice (with altered numbers as below).

> **TIP**
> To prevent any injuries, ensure that the circles will not slip as they are stepped onto. Try self-adhesive Velcro® on the back of each circle for carpeted areas, or white-tac on plastic-type flooring.

The dice
Make a dice to use with the stepping stones game, either with an ordinary dice or the 'Dice template page' on p. 133. Depending on how long you wish the game to last, change the numbers on the dice so that one and two are repeated, rather than five and six.

We played stepping stones many times and, to add variety to later games, we altered the dice to read 'Miss a turn', 'Go back one step', 'Whoops, you've slipped, start again' or 'Got wet feet, stay still'. The children actually loved to think up ways of not getting across the stream.

Method or how to play
1. Place the stones (card circles) a little distance apart from each other.
2. Take turns to throw the dice and move the appropriate steps across the stream.
3. Only one child on one stone is permitted (unless your stones are big enough to share).
4. The first child to reach the other side is the winner.

To add a bit of fun to the end, we allowed the winner to jump into the stream and paddle back to the beginning again, 'splashing' everyone still on stepping stones.

Try alternative versions with coloured stones and a colour dice to move across the stream. You may want to use only three colours and alter the dice accordingly, or add comments like 'Move to the next blue stone' or 'Jump over the next stone' to vary the game.

> **TIP**
> If floor space is limited and your stream narrow, use a dice with just one or two dots on it so that the game is not over too quickly.

Why not try the game outdoors? We used coloured plastic hula-hoops to get across the stream. The advantage of hoops is that more than one child can stand in them. One day, rather than use a dice, we threw beanbags into the hoops. As long as the beanbag landed in any hoop, the child could step over into it. Throwing and aiming skills improved tremendously!

Semi-circle fun

The 'Semi-circle activity page' is for comparing and matching, estimating and measuring.

The page can be photocopied, preferably onto card: cut out each semi-circle for use in any of the following activities. All the semi-circles have a matching half which will make a complete circle, the idea is to find the pairs.

Separate the semi-circles so that they are arranged haphazardly on a table. A child will need to look closely at each one and decide which seem to match. Once a pair has been spotted, they should be placed together to check whether or not a circle can be made with the two halves. Carry on until all the circles have been completed.

Is it easier to start by matching the biggest semi-circles? Or are the little circles quicker to spot than the bigger ones? Matching in this way is one method used in comparing and estimating.

Estimating size and length is a skill that can be enhanced by the following activities.

For estimating how long the diameters (the straight edges) of the semi-circles are before using rulers to measure accurately, cut strips of paper of varying lengths, some of which match the length of the diameter of the semi-circles. By looking carefully, the child chooses a strip of paper to match the diameter of a chosen circle from the table. If it is too short, they can add another strip to the first until the edges match or, if it is too long, cut a strip off one end to match the diameter. Repeat until the lengths match, adding or 'subtracting'.

Alternatively, ask the child to cut a length of string that they think will match the straight edge they have chosen. Once the string has been cut, compare the two and see how near to matching the string estimate has been.

Using small strips of paper, ask the child to choose two or three strips to a length equal to that of the diameter of one semi-circle. Lay them alongside the semi-circle's edge to check how accurate the estimate is, adding extra or taking away the surplus.

Measurements can take many forms. Already, using paper or string pieces, measuring has taken place. Rulers and measuring tapes in centimetres should only be used once children have an understanding of the process of measurement.

How many bricks laid end to end will be needed to match the biggest diameter? Will the smaller semi-circles need as many? How many fingers will fit along the smallest diameter? Try beads on a string or self-adhesive dots along the diameters to compare the different semi-circles.

There are endless possibilities!

Snap differences

When we started our circle project, we asked children and parents to take pictures of circles in their environment or cut out images from magazines and comics. We were absolutely amazed at the variety of photographs and pictures brought in.

There were many objects that were the same but also different. How many types of car wheels were produced, three or four? In actual fact we had over fifteen examples, including hub caps! There were several examples of road signs and manhole covers too. Parents supplied us with numerous buttons with two and four holes, all having different colours or designs. Up until that time I hadn't been aware of the sorts of sequins available either.

The whole idea started both Christine and I thinking about devising a game where there were two of the same item, but with different characteristics to match. Snap with a difference.

Which items to choose was our dilemma. We had so many photographs and pictures to choose from. We decided that although many of the objects were not technically circles, as they were three-dimensional, for the purpose of the game we would give ourselves a bit of leeway and chose two types of watch faces, bicycle wheels, buttons, biscuits, balls and road signs.

Playing the game

The game is played in exactly the same way as snap, except that each pair is of the same type of object but not necessarily an identical image.

Ingredients
One or more photocopies of the 'Snap differences game page' onto card, crayons (optional) and scissors.

Method
1. Colour the pictures or leave as black and white images.
2. Carefully cut out each individual picture to make the cards for the game.
3. Divide the cards equally between the players, placing the last card face-upwards on the table.
4. Turns are taken to place a card on top of that first card. If and when a matching object is spotted, whoever was first to say 'Snap' wins the cards.
5. The next player places a card face upwards on the table and play continues until one person has all the cards.

> **TIP**
> When playing with two or more sets there will be obvious matching pairs, but if playing with only one set of cards, ensure that any child playing understands the connections between the different images of the same object.

Snap differences game page

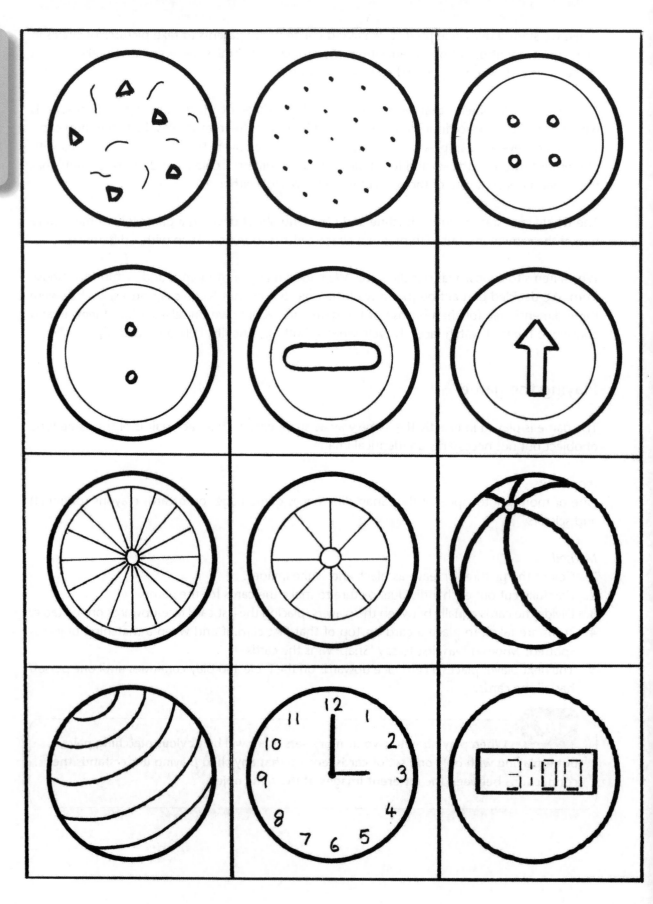

Section 3: Triangle

	KUW	CLL	PSRN	C	P	PSE
30 What's special about a triangle?	•	•	•	•		
31 A triangle of triangles		•	•	•	•	
32 A triangle of triangles activity page					•	
33 Triangular games		•	•	•	•	•
34 Triangular games page		•			•	
35 Camping corner	•	•		•		•
36 Street of roofs page		•				
37 Which fits where?	•	•	•	•	•	•

What's special about a triangle?

A triangle is one of the basic shapes of geometry. It is a polygon with three corners and three sides or edges. Each side can be a different length and the internal angles can be different too.

Triangles are named according to the lengths of their sides:

- An equilateral triangle has all the sides the same length so that it is a regular polygon with all the internal angles measuring 60°.
- An isosceles triangle has two sides of equal length and two angles that measure the same, the third angle and side being of a different measure.
- A scalene triangle has no sides the same length and all the internal angles are different from each other.

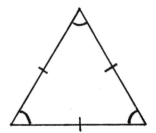  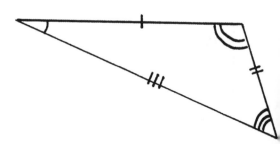

- A right-angled triangle has one internal angle of 90° (a right angle).
- An acute triangle has all of its internal angles less that 90°.
- An obtuse triangle has one internal angle that measures more than 90°.

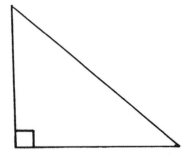 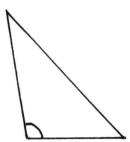 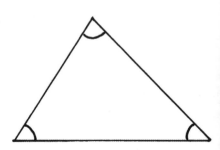

Triangles are special because of the diversity of their shape. Equilateral triangles put together make a diamond and six will make a hexagon. Try some tessellations to see!

The 'Triangle of triangles activity page' can be as complicated as you want to make it or as simple as can be. Each triangle within the triangle can be divided as often as required, making anything from a two-piece puzzle into one with over 250 pieces.

The main idea is to show how a triangle can be filled with triangles, often of different shapes which can be used as a puzzle, for colouring and counting activities, as a template, for tessellations or folding and making into three-dimensional objects.

The 'Triangle of triangles activity page' shows an equilateral triangle which has been divided into several other triangles as an example for you to adapt or use as it stands.

Inset puzzle

Ingredients
A photocopy on card, scissors or craft knife, ruler and cutting board (optional).

Method
1. Cut the photocopy in half. The large triangle outline will be the puzzle's base and can be cut out or left as it is.
2. Cut out the other triangles.
3. Now fit the triangles back into the big one again!

> **TIP** The cutting of the triangles needs to be as accurate as possible so that their sides match; this is probably best done by an adult. A craft knife, metal ruler and cutting board will help keep the lines straight.

Adapt the large equilateral triangle puzzle to suit each child:

- A simple two piece puzzle – cut the large triangle in half, from the top-most point to the middle of the bottom edge, making two right-angled triangles.
- A four piece puzzle – measure, divide and mark each side of the large triangle into two equal lengths. Draw lines from these halfway points to divide the triangle into four smaller equilateral triangles.
- Divide these four triangles further by making two right-angled triangles from one (as in the two piece puzzle), making five, six, seven or eight pieces, depending on whether or not each equilateral triangle is cut again.
- Divide the four equilateral triangles into four again to result in a seven, ten, thirteen or sixteen piece puzzle.
- Use a combination of right-angled and equilateral triangles to make a puzzle with anything from five to eight to 200-plus pieces.

The equilateral triangles can also be used as templates for making tessellations and pictures. Coloured paper and card will enhance the activities, or colour plain paper with paints, felt pens or crayons.

A triangle of triangles activity page

Triangular games

The 'Triangular games page' shows two games: the tepee and the snake. The ideas for both are interchangeable.

The tepee game

The tepee game is a colour matching activity although, with slight alterations, it can be played in various ways.

Colour matching
- If you have access to a colour photocopier: photocopy one tepee, colour each triangular section to correspond to the colours on a colour dice and then photocopy enough tepees for each child playing the game.
- If your photocopy is black and white: photocopy a tepee for each child playing the game and add colours to each triangle of the tepee, as above.

Take turns to throw the dice and place a white triangle or counter on a coloured triangle on the tepee to match the colour on the dice. Continue until all the triangle shapes are covered.

Number recognition
Rather than colouring each triangle, add a numeral to each space. Then, with an ordinary dice, play as above covering the appropriate numbers with a counter or cut-out triangle.

The whole idea can be made more complex by dividing each triangle into two or four.

The snake game

Added to the above activities are a few more to play with the snake outline.

Always ensure that a selection of cut-out triangles is available before playing the snake game. Older children may like to cut out their own triangles for each game.

A simple way of playing this game is to colour each section as the coloured dice is thrown. The triangles are small enough for each section to be crayoned before the child's turn comes round again. However, you may want to enlarge the image to produce bigger triangles to glue shapes to. The only rule we had was that any adjoining triangle could not be the same colour as the previous one, making a very colourful and striking snake.

For a quicker version of the game, we used an ordinary dice and glued the appropriate number of triangles onto the snake. The correct number had to be thrown at the end to reach the snake's head.

This makes a lovely game for the playground. It is very simple to draw and can be as long and twisting as space will allow. Numerals, dots or colours can be added to each triangular section and, together with the appropriate type of dice, an outdoor game can be played, involving all the children in your group.

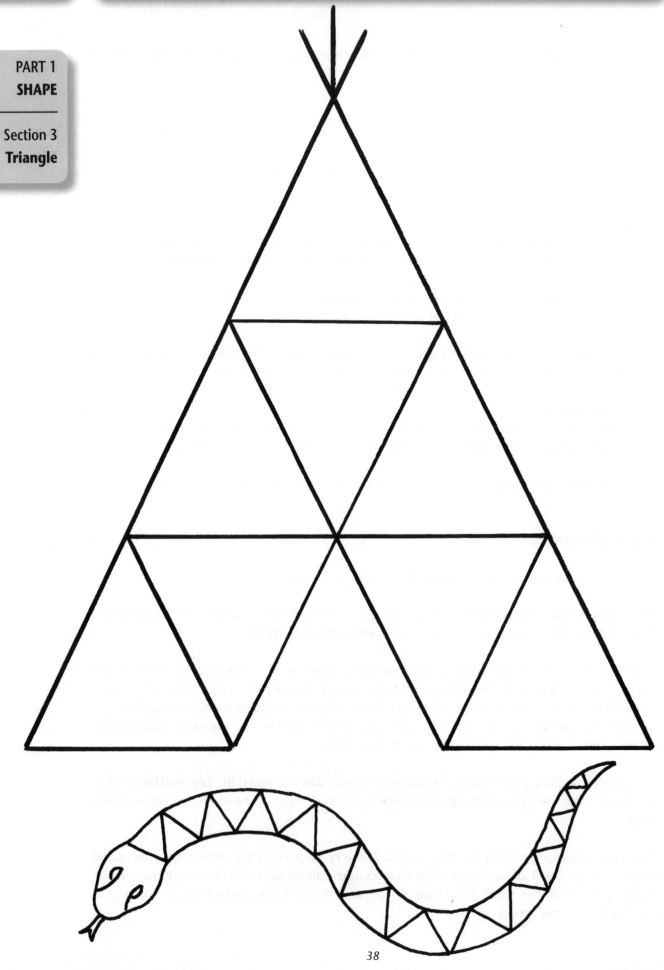

Camping corner

When we played the tepee game, the children wanted to make a real one to play inside. It fitted in with the triangle theme and seemed simple enough to accomplish at the outset.

I tried tying three or four bean poles with string, spreading them out and wrapping an old sheet around it. However, the finished construction was wobbly, to say the least. It looked good but certainly wouldn't stand up to any children playing in it, and had to be dismantled for safety reasons. The children were very disappointed, so we did the next best thing.

We made a tent with the sheet draped over a length of rope (skipping ropes work well) attached to a cupboard door handle and the windowsill. The sheet was spread apart so that the opening was triangular in shape and our camping corner was established. Little folding stools and table, an old camping stove and saucepan were borrowed from a parent. Squares of fabric were made into sleeping bags and our tent was ready for occupation.

One of our parents kindly offered to construct the tepee in the garden for us. He used more bean poles than we had had available and wedged them into the ground, which gave the tepee stability. It was a very popular addition to our outdoor play although it was used differently from the play house.

After discussing who actually lives in tepees, the children wanted to dress up like Native American Indians. They made jewellery with our beads and threads to wear. We also put some card weaving looms inside the tepee and the children added threads, fabric and paper to make colourful mats. The jewellery and mats were put on display in the same way that Native Americans sell their products.

The theme carried on in the art room where a settlement of tepees was constructed in the sandpit. A student helped the children make three-dimensional structures of tepees using kebab skewers (pointed ends removed), masking tape, crayons and paper.

The sides of the tepee were isosceles triangles which the children coloured with zig-zag patterns. Three kebab sticks were tied together and spread outwards to make the corners of a triangle and the patterned sides stuck to them with masking tape. This made the tepees quite secure. One of the sides had a triangle cut from it to make the door opening. When they were completed, other small world people and animals were added to the little campsite of tepees in the sand tray for another imaginative play activity.

Street of roofs page

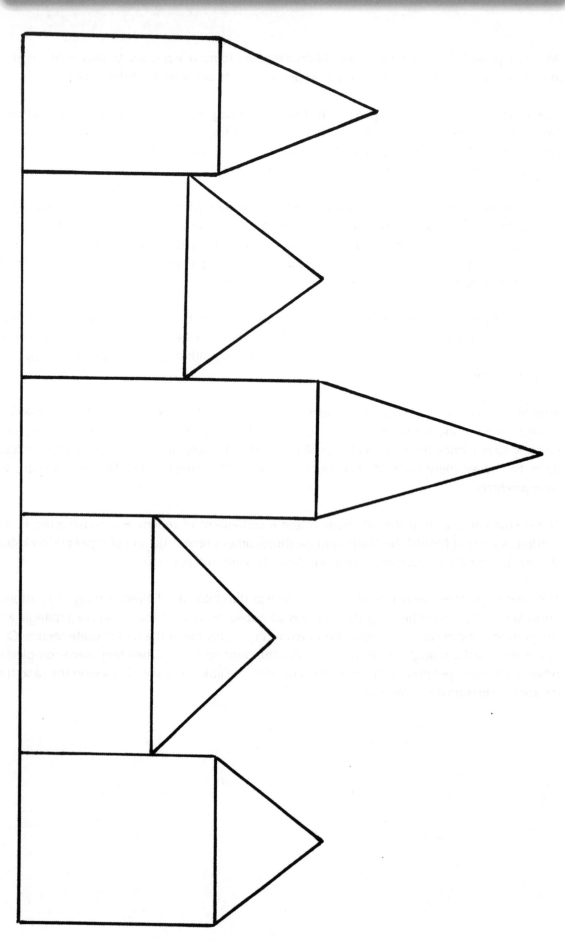

The 'Street of roofs page' came about when we were looking out of the windows at the skyline around our setting. The pre-school was situated at the edge of a car park in the middle of town, surrounded by all types of other buildings. Some had flat roofs but most were shaped. We were looking at the different chimney and roof shapes to develop the idea as a silhouette picture for a night-time skyline with a silvery moon as a display during our colour theme (see Part 2: Sections 9 and 10 for other ideas).

As the children were talking, we noticed how many different shaped triangles made up the roofs and the angles between roofs. The matching triangles to houses activity was devised from these observations.

Silhouette puzzle

Ingredients
A photocopy of the 'Street of roofs page', a sheet of black card, staples and stapler, and scissors.

Method
1. Staple the photocopy to a sheet of black card with the image uppermost.
2. Cut around the outer edge of the whole picture.
3. Leave the black silhouette in one piece and then cut along all the lines of the photocopy, making ten pieces.
4. These triangles and rectangles need to be placed onto the black shape of the street so that the houses and roofs match the outline.

Most puzzles with straight sides are more challenging than puzzles with curved or interlocking pieces. This puzzle is made more difficult because there are no colours to match a roof to a house or church.

Does colouring in the outlines help some children complete the game?

Some of the shapes have sides of equal length. Does that add difficulty to the puzzle?

If matching the shapes to the silhouette image is too difficult, photocopy the page again and use that as a base for matching the individual shapes.

Extend the activity by adding windows and doors to a photocopy of the original page. What about round windows? Or numbers on the doors?

Extend the activity, with the children making their own street design with triangles, squares and rectangles for their friends to try.

We made a display of 'our street' by cutting out large rectangles, squares and triangles. These were stuck onto sheets of A2 sugar paper. The children added 'lollipop' trees and flowers with triangular petals in the gardens. Triangular birds flew overhead and a cat sitting on a fence had rectangular whiskers! Some of the people were a little stiff looking but they all had arms and legs. One person had round hands with rectangular fingers. The display looked stunning when put together along the wall in the corridor.

Section 4: Square

	KUW	CLL	PSRN	C	P	PSE
38 What's special about a square?	•	•	•		•	
39 Page of squares					•	
40 All square but different	•		•	•	•	
41 A square of triangles	•	•	•		•	
42 Square of triangles activity page					•	
43 Construction site	•	•	•	•	•	•
44 Missing mortar maze		•			•	
45 A square meal	•	•		•		•

A square is a quadrilateral, a regular polygon, a rectangle, a parallelogram and a rhombus, all in one. That makes for a very special shape indeed.

- A quadrilateral is a flat shape with four sides and four angles or corners. A quadrilateral becomes a square when all the sides are the same length and the angles are all right angles.
- A regular polygon has sides that are equal in length and internal angles that are all the same.
- A rectangle has two sets of parallel sides. Opposite sides are the same length, one pair is longer than the other (except when it is a square, then all the sides are as broad as they are long). All internal angles are right angles of 90°. The diagonals bisect each other and are of equal length.
- A parallelogram has two sets of parallel sides. Opposite sides are the same length but one pair is longer than the other. Opposite angles are equal and their diagonals bisect. A square is a special example because its sides are always the same length, with all the angles equal.
- A rhombus has all four sides of equal length, the opposite sides are parallel and opposite angles are the same. It looks like a pushed over square. A square is a special example because the opposite angles are always 90°.

So a square is very special because all four sides are of equal length and opposite sides are parallel with four right angles. The diagonals perpendicularly bisect one another and are of equal length.

However, a polygon, rectangle, parallelogram and rhombus are not always squares!

Mosaics

One of the simplest mosaics to make is to fill a square with squares. We used a guillotine to cut strips of paper 2cm wide, and then again into 2cm squares. Squares easily tessellate and can make striking patterns or pictures. Cut squares from photographs, pictures from magazines and ordinary coloured paper for different effects.

Mosaic patterns were used extensively in Roman dwellings where they covered the surfaces of walls and floors. They are not necessarily made entirely from squares, as small fragments would be used to fill gaps in curved shapes.

Some of the children at our after-school club decided to make their own mosaics. They took a simple coloured image, drew a square grid over the top of it and then by using coloured paper squares, copied the picture in squares. Occasionally when one square showed different percentages of colour, they cut a square into four smaller squares so that the picture did not lose too much form.

TIP

Use cross-stitch patterns to provide ready-made 'mosaic' pictures.

Page of squares

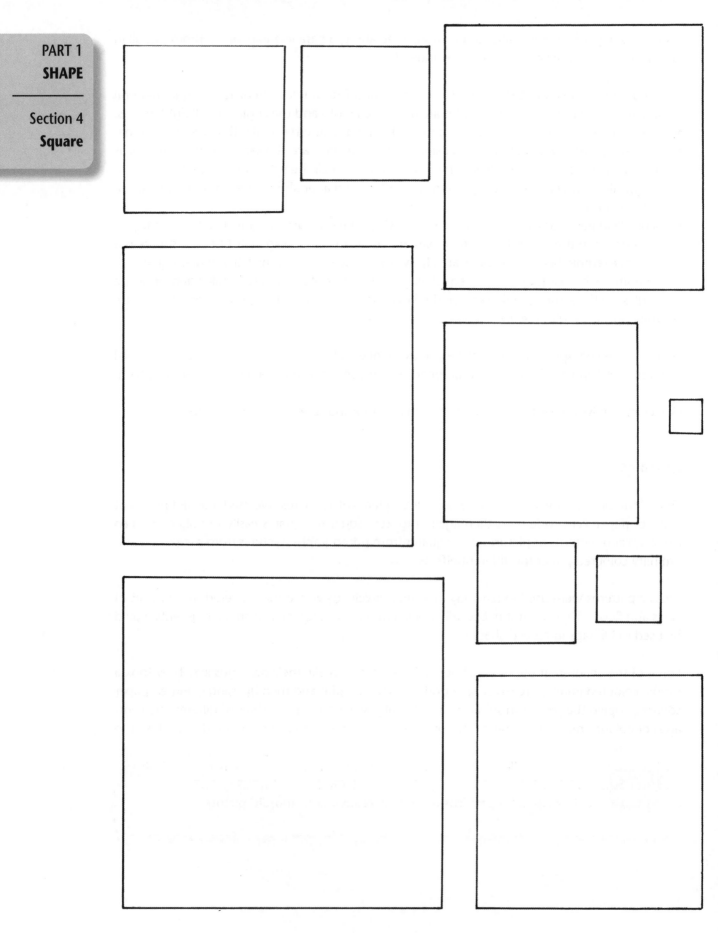

The 'Page of squares' came about when a child, who had been using wooden bricks to make a tessellating pattern, decided to see how many bricks it took to cover a sheet of paper.

The bricks measured about one and a half inches square. As he got towards the edge of the paper on the narrower side, there was a gap which he wanted to fill. The wooden bricks were too big, so he filled the space with some wooden cube beads. However, there was a larger gap at the top of the paper and the beads did not fill it. He chose some squared paper from the paper drawer and cut squares to fit along the edge.

Once the area was covered, he counted each type of 'square' and said, 'That's it done! Thirty-five bricks, that many beads and those squares cover one sheet of paper.'

This is how skills in mathematical measurement develop. He had made an equation without realising it.

I developed the idea later so that a page of squares could be used in lots of different ways.

Tessellating squares

As mentioned in previous activities, tessellating with squares is one of the simplest shapes to begin with. However, have you ever tried using squares of different sizes?

When the builders were laying paving slabs in the garden, I decided that it would be much more interesting if the slabs were of different sizes and formed a mosaic pattern. The slabs came in imperial measurements and were 30, 24, 18 and 12 inches square and the finished result was much more interesting to the children than uniform slabs.

Cut out four different sized squares from the 'Page of squares' and see the variety of patterns that can be created.

Square stairs

The 'Page of squares' can be used as it stands for estimating which is the biggest, right down to the smallest. We numbered each one as a child indicated them in size order. When they were cut out and placed in numerical order on the table, 'swaps' had to be made to ensure the squares descended in order of size.

Try beginning with the smallest square and work up to the largest. Is one way easier to achieve than the other? What happens if you use different coloured paper squares? Do some squares appear to be bigger or smaller than they were on white paper?

Try the same idea with rectangles, changing the size in length only. Then try it by widening the rectangle.

Do parallelograms and rhombus work as well?

A square of triangles

The 'Square of triangles activity page' can be used as a puzzle of two or more pieces. The square can be divided in half across a diagonal to make a two-piece puzzle.

As with the triangle of triangles, ensure that there is a base shape of the same size for a child to fit each piece on top of the other as a guide.

Cutting across both diagonals will produce a four-piece puzzle which consists of four right-angled triangles. Many children will begin to fit the pieces onto the base outline by matching the right angle of a triangle to a right-angle in the square. They will then place another triangle along the long side of the first triangle, as they did with the two-piece puzzle. The two pieces produce another square which is much smaller than the base shape, with two triangles left over.

Encourage a child to experiment with these four triangles. Several different sized shapes can be found.

What will happen if all the right-angles of the triangles are put in the corners of the base square so that the pieces overlap slightly?

Discard the base shape and see what shapes can be made.

What do you see if the triangles are joined by two short sides, then two long sides, then two short sides again?

Which shape is made by joining two long sides together, then two short sides and then two long sides?

Giving children the opportunity to experiment in this way will help to begin the process of understanding the properties of shapes and ultimately how angles work.

These four triangles can be cut again to make smaller right-angled triangles. This increases the difficulty in finding how they all fit together to make the base shape, but also increases the number of ways it can be achieved. The 'Square of triangles activity page' gives just four examples, and the more triangles you cut into right-angled triangles, the more patterns and arrangements can be made.

We also tried a square of squares page. Instead of making a puzzle by cutting across the diagonal, we cut across the middle of the square both ways to make four smaller squares, i.e. we bisected each side of the original square. As with the idea above, one or two of these squares were then divided into four more squares.

We used them as a puzzle but also for tessellating patterns. Cut out squares in assorted colours of paper and make mosaic patterns and pictures too. Refer to 'All square but different' for another idea.

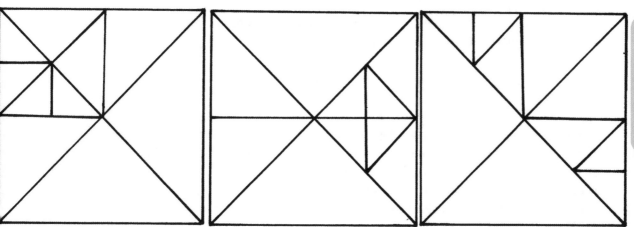

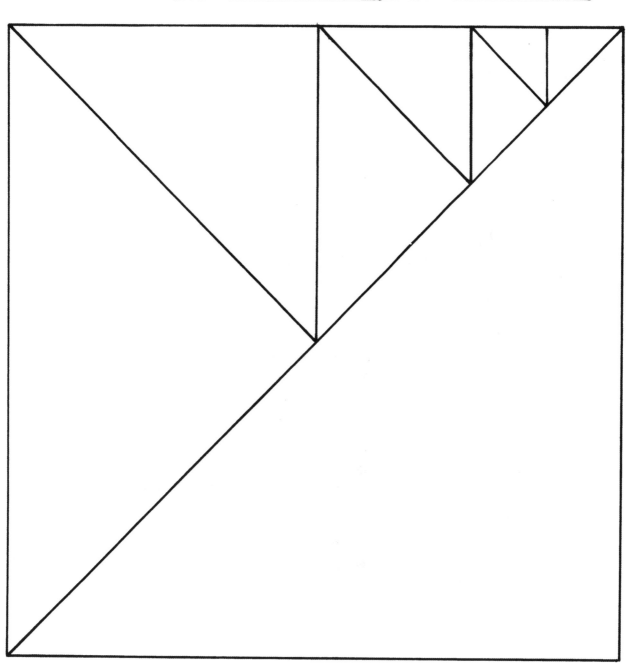

Construction site

These ideas actually came to life after the builders had been to lay our new paving slabs in the garden (as mentioned in 'All square but different').

Outdoors

The children used buckets and spades, trowels and rakes in the sand pit to re-enact the busy builders. We had some brick moulds which they used as paving slabs initially. Then one of our staff team remembered some foam board she had used at college which she cut into squares as paving slabs. With wet sand as the mortar, the children laid a 'patio' in the sand tray. With a small spirit level (and adult supervision) the slabs were as flat as a pancake and did not wobble at all.

Creative

We transferred the idea to the art room too. We mixed PVA glue into some damp sand, and with squares of thick card, paving slabs were laid with gusto! The children spread the stiff mixture with spatulas (trowels) onto card and then placed the squares on top, leaving a slight gap between each one to make a patio, a more unusual type of mosaic or tessellation.

Play corner

This became a 'proper' building site. Now the children knew how to lay patios, they tried their hand at building walls. One large area of a room seemed to be taken over with groups of children building with old wooden bricks, Duplo®, large plastic hollow bricks and boxes. Hard hats were worn, sand toys were borrowed from the sand pit and cups of tea were drunk by the gallon!

> **TIP**
> Try to keep activities like this on a carpeted area or mats, as the toppling of towers and brick walls can be very noisy and distracting in a room where other, quieter, activities are taking place.

Missing mortar maze

The idea for the maze happened by chance when one little boy, playing on the new slabs, suddenly shouted, 'Hey, they've missed a bit, the weeds will grow through where there's no cement!' An experience from home, or perhaps a future builder?

Christine and I looked at the paving slabs that had been laid and noticed a couple of small gaps in the mortar. What a good idea, the pattern was already drawn and with a few more missing bits of mortar, a ready-made maze sprang to mind. That's not to say we removed more bits of cement from between the slabs, but we did use it as a template for our 'Missing mortar maze' page. With this maze, as a child finds her way through, she fills in the gaps as she goes.

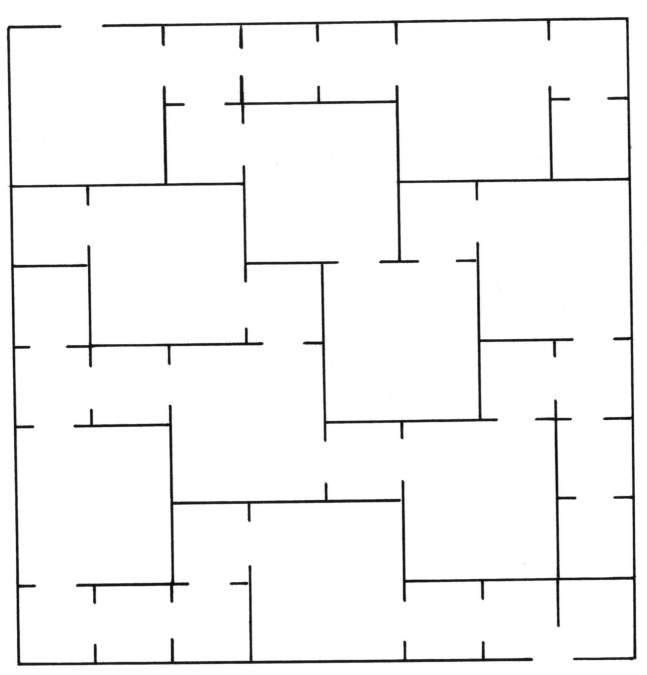

A square meal

There are a number of sayings that refer to geometric shapes, e.g. the 'family circle', an 'eternal triangle' and 'back to square one'.

When it comes to squares there are plenty of phrases to choose from. 'He won it fair and square' suggests there was no cheating or fixing of the match or game. 'A square peg in a round hole' usually refers to something or somebody which does not fit in, a misfit. Whereas 'a square dance' refers to a dance in which four pairs of partners face each other in a square and keep to that area throughout the dance.

But the phrase that always fascinated me was 'a square meal'. Whenever I came home from college my mum would always have a square meal ready for me. It was never on a square plate, like on board ship in the Royal Navy, nor was it made up of square things. To my mum it meant a nourishing, substantial and satisfying meal!

Why not have a square meal at nursery, I thought, with square food? Our cook was ever inventive and gave it a go. She used the square-shaped cake tin (although it did have slightly rounded edges) to make a delicious cheese and potato pie which she divided into square portions. It was accompanied by diced carrots and swede. For dessert we had sultana flapjacks cut into squares.

Our snacks followed the theme that week too. We poured orange and apple juice into ice-cube trays to eat, suck or put in drinks later in the week. When they had been eaten we used the trays to make individual jellies as a treat.

We had square sandwiches filled with square slices of ham or cheese.

Many square crackers had rounded corners but were still tasty eaten with cubes of cheese.

We borrowed (and thoroughly cleaned) the square cutters we used for play-dough activities and made several types of square biscuits, the most popular being shortcake squares.

We used these square cutters to make small cheese scones which were absolutely delicious and took very little time to make.

Ingredients
170g self-raising flour, 28g margarine, 85g grated cheese, 1 beaten egg, 2 tbsp milk, salt, pepper and mustard powder to taste, a rolling pin and square cutters.

Method
1. Rub the margarine into the flour, add cheese and seasoning.
2. Add the egg and milk.
3. Roll out on a floured board to 1cm thickness and cut into squares.
4. Brush the tops with egg or milk, sprinkle with a little grated cheese.
5. Bake in a hot oven (225°C, Gas mark 7–8) for 15 minutes.

Eat and enjoy within two days.

Section 5: Pentagon

	KUW	CLL	PSRN	C	P	PSE
46 What's special about a pentagon?	•	•	•	•		
47 Page of pentagons		•				
48 The Pentagon	•		•	•		•
49 Pentagon maze					•	
50 A pentagon of triangles		•	•	•	•	
51 Pentagon of triangles puzzle page					•	
52 Pentagon game		•			•	•
53 Pentagonal paper painting				•	•	•

In geometry, a pentagon is any five-sided polygon. It may be a simple polygon or one of a more complex nature whose lines intersect. As mentioned in Section 1: Unusual two dimensions, use five strips to make pentagons. The 'Page of pentagons' will give you some designs, how many more can you devise?

What happens when you use strips that are all different lengths?

What effects are made by having two long strips and three short ones?

Does the order in which they are joined make for differing shapes?

What happens when the strips are all the same length?

A pentagon is regular when all its sides are the same length and all its internal angles are the same, but they can be quite tricky to draw accurately.

Here is one way of working out the internal angles of a regular shape so that they can be easily drawn with accuracy, using the internal angles of a triangle to help.

1. Divide the shape into triangles from one corner (vertex) so that they do not overlap.
2. Count the number of triangles in the shape and multiply that by 180°, as each triangle has internal angles of 180°.
3. Then divide that figure by the number of sides the shape has. The result will be the internal angle of the regular shape you want to draw.

Following the steps above, work out the internal angles of a regular pentagon.

A regular pentagon can be divided into three triangles that do not overlap, starting at one vertex (corner). Multiply 3 by 180° = 540°. Then divide 540° by 5 (the number of sides to a pentagon) = 108°.

Start by drawing a line the length of the side for the pentagon required. Place a protractor at the end to make an angle of 108° and draw another side. Carry on until the five sides are measured and added. They should join up to be a regular pentagon.

Try the method above to make a square or regular hexagon.

This may seem a very difficult task for our early years' children. However, I was showing some children at our holiday club how to make a regular pentagon because our template was missing, when a younger child joined the group. He was four years old and wanted to know what we were up to. He had seen a protractor in his much older brother's pencil case and wanted to know how to use it. With supervision and encouragement from the schoolchildren, he made a very good attempt at drawing a regular pentagon and enjoyed the experience of being with the older children too!

The Pentagon

A very famous building in the United States of America is The Pentagon. It is a government building with five sides and is the headquarters of the country's Department of Defense. The children and I were discussing how the rooms in our two-storey nursery were linked: by stairs and corridors, hallways and doors. Sometimes 'new' children needed help to find the bathroom or cloakroom because the layout of the building was unfamiliar to them.

This got us all wondering how difficult it would be to find your way around a five-sided building which must be full of rooms, cupboards and a maze of corridors going in different directions.

We decided to 'have a go' at making a maze on the playground outside. With chalk in hand we started with the outside shape. The first few lines were about four metres long and then gradually became shorter as, without lifting the chalk, we carried on drawing lines towards the middle of the pentagon, keeping its shape throughout. Several sticks of chalk and a couple of grazed knuckles later and we had created a 'spiral' type maze. The children loved the idea of following the line to the centre, and we carried on the American theme by drawing a star (from their flag) in the middle.

We all enjoyed the activity so much that the children each chose a paving slab to draw their own versions of The Pentagon. It was a good job that we had a full box of chalk sticks!

The activity had been so successful that Christine and I decided to make a more challenging maze on paper rather than the basic spiral patterns chalked outside.

Initially, because we were associating the maze with The Pentagon building in America, Christine drew 'rooms' in the blocked areas of the 'corridors'. There were little images of items we thought may be behind the closed doors of government office buildings: filing cabinets, tables and chairs, maps and notice boards, computers and telephones. However, the path through the maze was so obvious that the enjoyment of twisting and turning to find a way to the centre was spoilt. So although we dispensed with the rooms, you can add them to make the maze easier for younger children.

Several children added rooms after finding their way to the star, and some of their pictures gave us an insight into their understanding of office life. The one maze that stuck in my mind were the little cups drawn in several places – Ryan's mum worked in an office in town and loved her cups of coffee apparently!

A pentagon of triangles

At one of the pre-schools where I worked there was a wooden inset puzzle of a pentagon. It contained 25 isosceles triangles. The pieces were three differently sized triangles and when they were all placed in the wooden inset an empty pentagonal shape was left in the centre. The puzzle was beautifully made but was one of the most difficult to complete.

Christine and I decided to recreate a similar puzzle but with simpler lines where the triangles all centre around the middle of the pentagon, without the empty pentagon shape. Cut out a pentagon shape (the same size as the one on the 'Pentagon of triangles puzzle page') as the base to enable children to place each of the triangles within an outline.

Start with only five triangles of identical size and shape. As the children gain confidence in filling the outline, they may like to cut one of the triangles in half to make two right-angled triangles; and by cutting each original triangle in the same way, a ten-piece puzzle can be made.

These triangles can obviously be divided further, making the puzzle much more complex. When we first tried the activity with a small group of children, we found that drawing five lines on the base shape, from the centre to each point of the pentagon, helped them to visualise how the triangles could fit into the spaces.

What happens if the original triangles are cut differently? Is the puzzle made more difficult? Turn the triangles out from the base shape so that the edges of the triangles match with the base shape and see what happens.

Can the triangles be used to make other patterns or pictures? Are more triangles needed to add extra details? What can be achieved with different types of triangles?

A five-pointed star
1. Measure one-quarter of the way up each line of symmetry on a regular pentagon and make a small mark.
2. Draw lines from each of those marks to the nearest points (or corners) of the pentagon.
3. Cut along those ten lines (cutting out five isosceles triangles) – what shape have you made?

Templates and dot-to-dot
Use this star as a template and for making a dot-to-dot activity.

1. Place the star on a piece of paper.
2. Draw a dot at each point and trough.
3. Number each dot from one to ten.

Refer to other activities in *Activities for Individual Learning through Rhyme*, Part 2: Section 7: Twinkle Twinkle Little Star, published by Continuum, 2010.

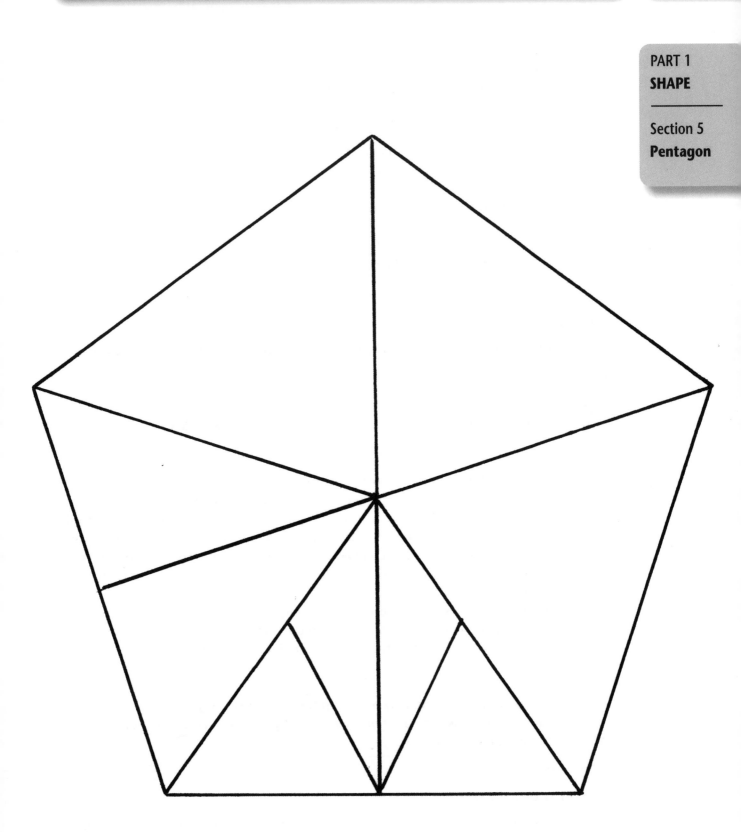

Pentagon game

How you play these games will depend on the number of children in your setting and how many children want to play. The games can be mixed together to make another activity or your children may invent some additional ideas to enhance their enjoyment.

Five fingers, five toes

Each child or team of five thinks of something to do with five fingers or toes. Each side takes turns to say and perform one thing they can do with their fingers or toes; e.g. tickle their friend, do a high five or stand on tip-toe. If an idea is repeated, that team has to do a forfeit to do with five; e.g. find five toy cars, count to five or jump up and down five times, etc.

> **TIP**
>
> This is quick to do at the end of a day or as a filler between activities.

Five not out

This is a much simplified version of baseball and needs two teams of five, five beanbags and a bucket.

> **TIP**
>
> Younger children find a hoop an easier target than a bucket.

1. Place five chairs at intervals around an area for running.
2. The first player from one team stands in between two chairs to start with and begins to throw the five beanbags into the bucket. Each beanbag in the bucket accounts for a run to the next chair. Five beanbags will mean the player can run all the way round the course passing every chair, back to the beginning, scoring one point for their team. So if a child throws one beanbag into the bucket, he will run to the first chair and sit down, waiting for the next player to throw.
3. As the next player throws, any team member sitting on a chair must run the appropriate number of runs between chairs to correspond to the number of beanbags thrown into the bucket. Any player reaching the start again wins a point for their team.

> **TIP**
>
> The team waiting to play picked up the beanbags ready for the next thrower and often they liked to position themselves by a chair to remind the other team how many chairs to run past.

Five-star memory game

We based this idea on the 'When I went shopping I bought a . . .' memory game. It happened quite by accident when, during one music session, I couldn't remember the song about five fishes. So I suggested that each child chose a rhyme or song about five that we could sing. The list got longer and longer, and if the parents hadn't arrived to collect their children, we would have continued well into the evening!

During a theme of shapes at one pre-school, we concentrated on the creative aspect connected with shapes. We had tried bubble painting for circles, making tent pictures with triangles, mosaics with squares, but when it came to pentagons we were at a bit of a loss. Regular pentagons do not tessellate and ones that do are quite difficult for under-fives to draw, so what to do?

'How about us having a pentagon competition?' suggested one of our after-schoolers. 'Just give us all a piece of paper and we'll come up with some good ideas.'

He used a sheet of A2 sugar paper which he cut so that it had five straight sides. 'Here's my first pentagon.' Then he took a stick of chalk and drew five thick lines by using the length of the stick rather than the end. The lines did not overlap. He then drew two more pentagons in other colours. Finally he took a chalk eraser and 'drew' five lines across the paper, smudging some of the previous lines, blending the chalk. The result was unusual and effective.

With the younger children we cut the paper into a pentagon shape for them and left them to paint, crayon and chalk pentagons on their pictures. When a child spilt a pot of water onto her picture, the colours blended instantly in some places and this led us to experiment further.

We painted on damp paper to see if the colours would blend more effectively and eventually found that the thicknesses and types of paper often required different amounts of water on them for the colours to mix well.

Colour-washes worked very well, even on dry paper, and although the pentagons became less clear, the display we made with all our experimental pictures was very colourful.

Printing pentagons

Printing with shapes can be done in several ways. In the 1970s when I started my career, we shaped potatoes or cut shapes from cork board which we then stuck onto wood blocks or corks. Nowadays there are a number of craft items that can be cut with scissors or craft knives and used for printing blocks; form board and funky foam are two examples that are readily available at most art and craft retailers as well as from educational catalogues. Once the shapes have been cut, glue them to card and attach to corks or blocks for printing.

We attached foam shapes to the tubes from kitchen roll, painted over them and rolled the tubes over paper to make a continuous pentagon pattern. Try textured wallpaper around a tube for a similar effect.

Section 6: Hexagon

	KUW	CLL	PSRN	C	P	PSE
54 What's special about a hexagon?		•	•	•		•
55 Find the queen bee maze page					•	
56 Bee amazed	•	•		•	•	
57 Bee keeping	•	•			•	•
58 Hexagon of triangles activity page					•	
59 Hexagon of triangles	•		•	•		•
60 Join the dots		•	•	•		•
61 Join the dots activity page					•	

A hexagon is a polygon with six edges and six vertices. Vertices are the corners where two sides of a shape meet. A regular hexagon has six sides of the same length and internal angles of the same size – 120°. How to work out the size of the angles in a regular hexagon has been explained in the previous section, 'What's special about a pentagon?'.

Hexagonal display

To make a colourful display of hexagons use strips of paper, collage materials and lots of imagination. Each child is given six different lengths of paper measuring one to two centimetres wide, a sheet of paper and a stick of glue.

The only rule is that each end of a strip must touch the end of another strip to make a hexagon. The lines may overlap to make as many as five spaces or they may zigzag across the page, as long as the ends join up.

Experiment with the positions of the strips before sticking them in place. Once they are stuck down, decorate the inner areas with collage materials. We used all sorts of paper, fabric, threads and sequins. Some children preferred to crayon or paint in the shapes. Once the pictures were dry, we cut around the perimeter of each hexagon and mounted them against a contrasting background paper onto a notice board in the main room of the nursery. It didn't have a calming effect, however, due to the busyness of the colours and shapes, but it did cause a lot of chatter, comparing different shapes and colours made from just six strips of paper.

Extend the activity by changing the coloured strips of paper to thinner black ones stuck to acetate. Decorate with tissue paper pieces to resemble stained-glass windows.

Tessellation with triangles

Regular hexagons tessellate well, add different colours to make patterns and pictures.

> **TIP**
> Save time drawing by using the 'Find the queen bee maze page', delete the bees and complete the hexagons.

Add equilateral triangles (with sides the same length as the regular hexagon) to make more elaborate patterns.

By playing around with irregular hexagons we found that many tessellate with the addition of triangles or four-sided polygons. There was plenty of trial and error involved; slivers of paper cut carefully from the sides of shapes, more often whole sides being snipped away making pentagons instead. However, none of these pieces were wasted; they were put in our collage boxes for another activity and another day!

> **TIP**
> Once we found two or three shapes that worked, we cut out several together, saving time. See 'Tips and shortcuts' for more information.

Find the queen bee maze page

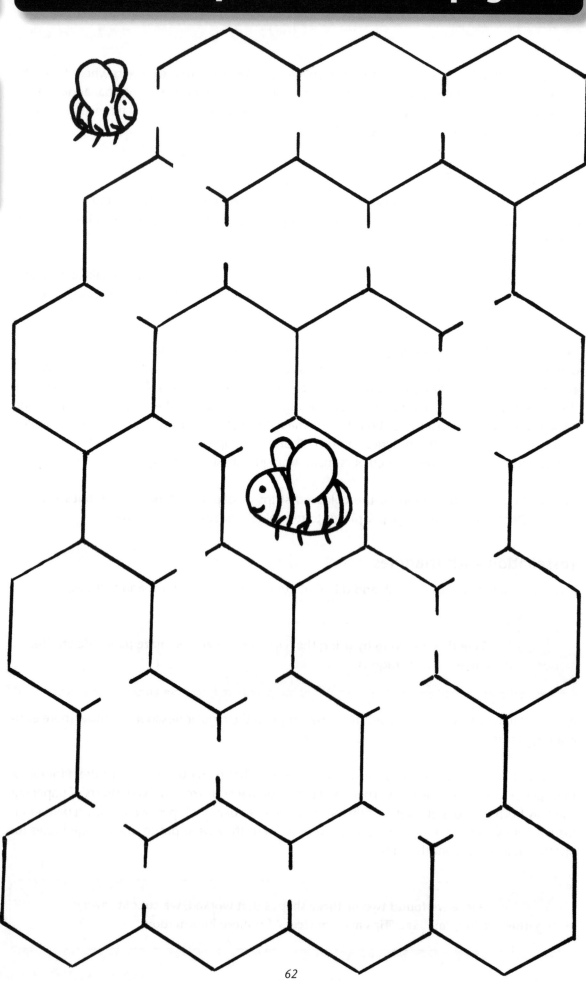

Bee amazed

The maze is based on the idea of how bees make natural tessellations of hexagons in their honeycombs within a beehive. These hexagon shapes are called cells and contain eggs and larvae as well as honey and wax.

A domesticated bee colony is housed in a rectangular hive. This usually has eight to ten parallel vertical frames which can be removed by the beekeeper to extract the honey and wax which is often found in the outer two frames. The inner frames contain the eggs, larvae, pupae and food for the colony, with honey stored towards the outer edges. Some hives have a separate brood box below these frames for the queen bee to lay her eggs in cells away from the main honey chamber.

The maze was devised with the queen bee in the centre for the other bee to find her and feed her larvae, depositing honey as she goes. Eleanor loved bees and honey and wanted first go at completing the maze. She chose an orangey-yellow crayon to trace the path to the queen, and every blocked hexagon she filled with colour to represent the honey. Eleanor seemed to know a great deal about bees and beekeeping and we soon found out how and why.

She knew that beekeepers wear clothes to protect themselves from bee stings but that her uncle often got stung by his bees. He didn't always wear his gloves so that he could handle the frames inside each hive more easily.

The clothing is usually light in colour and consists of long-sleeved gloves, a hooded suit, a hat and a veil. Bees are wary of dark colours because their natural predators are bears and skunks which are usually dark brown or black. Protective clothing is sensibly light so as not to cause bees' natural instincts to be aroused.

A colony of bees consists of tens of thousands of insects, but only one queen. All the female worker bees and the male drones are the queen bee's offspring and she may live for over three years. She can produce thousands of eggs during her lifetime, sometimes laying as many as 2,000 a day.

However, the female worker bees may only live for up to six weeks as their work is often non-stop through the busy summer season. They clean the cells (hexagons), incubate the queen's eggs, feed the larvae, receive the honey and pollen from the field bees, build cells and make wax.

The male drone bees are the largest bees in the hive and do not work or collect pollen or nectar. They are only produced to mate with queen bees.

Bee keeping

We were very lucky to have the opportunity to show the children an actual honeycomb in a frame taken from a hive. A few days after Eleanor had told us about her uncle's bees, she brought in two jars of honey from him. One was quite runny and the other more crystallised, but both smelt delicious.

The children spread them on bread, toast or crackers at snack time and decided that both honeys tasted as good as they smelt. Our cook used some of each to make flapjacks and a special biscuit she called yummy runny honeys (melting moments, I think). We ate those at lunchtime and sent a few home for Eleanor's uncle, to say 'Thank you' for our treat.

The following week we had an even greater surprise. Eleanor arrived at nursery accompanied by her uncle with his protective clothing on (even his gloves). He also brought in a frame from a hive he was cleaning out ready to introduce a new queen bee and colony of bees to it. The frame had empty cells in it as well as cells filled with honey and sealed with wax. The children were fascinated by the fact that the honey was solid and not runny.

Eleanor's uncle explained that when the bees place the honey in the cells it is very wet from their saliva. The bees fan their wings to dry the honey and thicken it. Then they seal the cell with a plug or layer of wax until the honey is eaten by the colony or removed to be eaten by us. The wax produced from a gland on the bee's abdomen is near its stinger and its colour varies from white to yellow to brown depending on the type of flowers the bees visit. Apparently the wax is similar to the wax secretion in our ears.

The honey from this hive was lavender flavoured and a pale orange colour. Eleanor's uncle mentioned that bees often travel up to two miles to reach the lavender flowers and eat the nectar from them. Then they use enzymes in their saliva to break the nectar down into sugars (honey) which is stored in the cells.

When beekeepers extract the honey from the frames, they scrape or cut off the wax caps to use later, along with the wax honeycomb.

The children asked him all sorts of pertinent questions related to bee keeping, and we spent a very informative and pleasant morning with him. He also sang his favourite song to us all, made famous by Arthur Askey – 'The Busy Bee'.

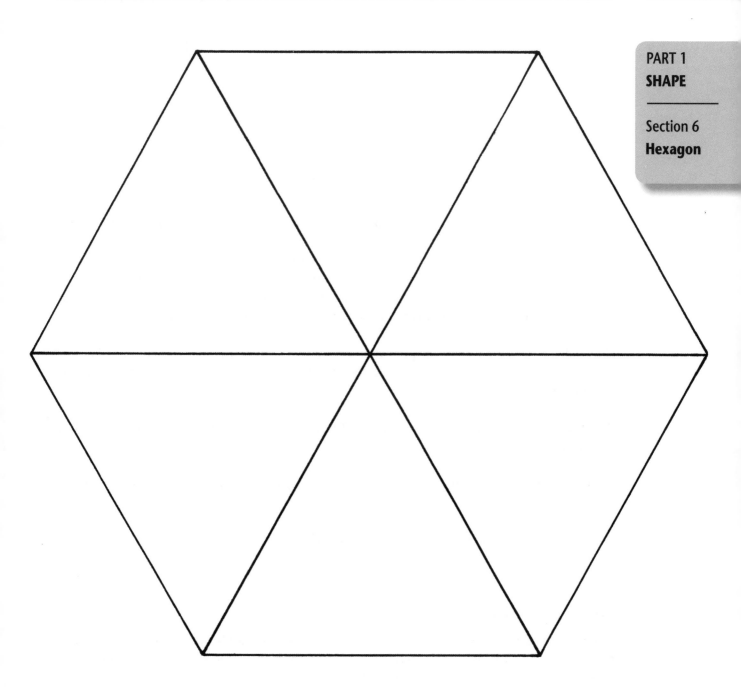

Hexagon of triangles

The 'Hexagon of triangles activity page' can be used as a spinner as well as a shape puzzle.

Puzzle

Ingredients

A photocopy of the 'Hexagon of triangles activity page', a second plain sheet of paper and scissors.

Method

1. Place the sheet of paper behind the photocopy and cut out the hexagon shape through both sheets.
2. Cut the hexagon into six triangles, making a quick and simple puzzle.
3. The plain sheet is the base in which to fit the triangular pieces to make the puzzle.
4. As the six pieces are all equilateral triangles, with sides the same length as the sides of the hexagon, the pieces will fit in any space whichever way they are turned.

How difficult does the puzzle become when one or two of these triangles are cut in half to make two right-angled triangles? Try cutting all the pieces into right-angled triangles and fitting them into the hexagon outline.

What happens if one equilateral triangle is cut into four smaller equilateral triangles as with the triangle of triangles puzzle?

Try the same idea with an irregular hexagon and its outline. Are these shapes easier to fit together?

What other pictures can be made with these different triangles? Is it possible to make a rectangle or square?

Spinner choices

A spinner can take the place of an ordinary dice if numerals are added or as a replacement colour dice when each segment is coloured. We also used them for other ideas and games described in *Activities for Individual Learning through Rhyme* (Continuum, 2010).

Ingredients

Photocopies onto card, crayons, felt pens, scissors and a pencil.

Method

1. Cut out the hexagonal shape.
2. Add numerals or colours as required.
3. Pierce the centre with a sharp pointed pencil and push the pencil through the middle so that when the pencil top is twisted, the hexagon will spin around. The spinner is now ready for use in any game requiring a six-sided dice.

TIP Always supervise activities well when using sharp implements to pierce holes in card or paper, even pencils can be dangerous in certain circumstances.

Use ideas from Part 2: Section 1 of this book where circular spinners are made. What effects can be achieved by colouring or decorating the triangles in different ways on a hexagonal spinner?

Make a spinner for outdoor activity choices, e.g. add pictures or photographs of equipment and toys you have available. The children use the spinner to decide which activity they will take part in, or hide the items that appear on the spinner for the children to find around the playground or garden.

The 'Join the dots activity page' started life as an aid to a few younger children who wanted to draw a hexagon but found that using a template to draw around was too difficult for them. They were developing their manipulative skills and hand–eye co-ordination but wanted to participate in an activity with older and more able children, so we suggested that they hold the template with one hand, mark the six corners with a pencil in their other hand, then remove the template and join the dots to make their hexagon.

They loved the idea of joining the dots and, when the other children saw them drawing 'freehand', they joined in too. One of the older children had used a ruler to extend the lines of their hexagon and showed that when the lines overlapped, it made a six-pointed star. There was our join the dots!

Initially we left several sheets of the dots on a table for individual children to play around with ideas rather than number the dots in order to make the star.

Some children made patterns, some made little triangles. Try some of their ideas and the join the dots activity becomes more than a six-pointed star.

By using some of the dots twice, make two large equilateral triangles.

Join all the dots to make six small equilateral triangles as well as a hexagon. Do you have to use some dots more than once?

Use all the dots to make four triangles, without using any dots twice. Are the triangles all the same shape? Are the triangles joined together or separate?

Join up the six outer dots in order. What shape is made? Join up the inner dots in order. Is it a different shape?

Hopscotch hexagons

Hopscotch is usually drawn as squares with chalk on a playground. But after seeing regular hexagon tessellations, we gave hopscotch a new look. We made a template from a cardboard box and used it to make our hopscotch board.

We played the game exactly as ordinary hopscotch, writing the numerals in each shape and hopping when there was one hexagon, and landing with one foot in each shape when there were two hexagons side by side. However, the marker we played with was slightly different from our usual flat stone. An NNEB student, on placement with us, made the children a hexagonal beanbag especially for the game.

The idea of hexagon hopscotch was added to her portfolio and she left the beanbag with us when she moved on to another placement.

Join the dots activity page

Section 7: Sphere

	KUW	CLL	PSRN	C	P	PSE
62 What's special about a sphere?	•	•				•
63 Find the spheres activity page	•	•				
64 Making spheres	•			•	•	•
65 Shopping for spheres		•	•	•	•	•
66 Get the ball rolling		•		•	•	•
67 Which marble makes it?		•			•	•
68 Which marble makes it maze	•				•	
69 Blowing bubbles	•	•	•	•	•	

What's special about a sphere?

A sphere is a three-dimensional, perfectly round geometrical object. Just like a two-dimensional circle, a perfect sphere is completely symmetrical around its centre. Every point on the surface of a sphere is the same distance away from its centre which is called the radius, as in a circle. The diameter of a sphere passes through its centre and is twice the length of its radius.

When we were looking for circular objects during our topic, we came across many shapes around us: manhole covers, our local lollipop lady's sign and traffic lights. Is finding spheres in the local environment more difficult than finding circles?

During several walks to the shops, park and library, the children and members of staff looked very carefully to find as many spherical objects as they could. It wasn't at all easy.

In the park, children spotted some berries in a hedge and later saw a different type on a tree. Both were spherical and different shades of brilliant red. Some of the berries were picked by an adult (with gloves on in case the berries were poisonous) and brought back to identify. One group of berries was from a rowan or mountain ash tree and are a favourite food of birds, the other berries were from bindweed growing over a hawthorn hedge, which produces berries later on in the year.

The children who walked to the local shops spotted a Belisha beacon at each end of the zebra-crossing in the middle of town. They found lots of other shapes on the church building next to the crossing. The clock face was circular, the sun dial had a triangular indicator and the stained-glass windows were full of shapes. However, as they were passing, one of the children noticed the lights on inside; they were all globes, very spherical, and well spotted by Lisa!

The children at the library found their task even more difficult. However, they did return with two books about shapes which, on looking through, only added marbles, a globe and balls to our quest for spheres.

Finding spheres was not an easy task, especially when one child pointed out that our globe had lumps and bumps on the surface (where the mountain ranges were), so it couldn't be a sphere either. Help!

Find the spheres activity page

After discussing whether or not the world is spherical because our globe had lumps and bumps on it, we decided that the only way we could find more spheres was to make them ourselves.

With Christine's 'Find the spheres activity page', all the objects suggest they are three-dimensional (whereas, because they are drawn, they are flat and are technically two-dimensional) and the idea is to decide whether or not each item would be a sphere if held. Most children took the activity at face value and included the globe and the jar of sweets. However, two children decided that although the lollipop had a spherical sweet top, the stick meant it was not a sphere and did not include it in their findings. One little boy coloured only two of the spherical sweets in the jar because he could see they were completely round. He said the others could be chipped like the rhubarb and custard sweets he had had. They were just like the ones in the picture but lots of them were broken and not spherical.

I loved the fact that these children were using their powers of observation, thinking skills and making judgements accordingly.

Making clay spheres

Spheres can be made from play-dough or clay. There is some lovely colourful modelling clay available in craft shops and educational catalogues, although play-dough is cheap and easy to make. Always read the instructions carefully before using modelling clay as some types require cooking in an oven on a low heat, whereas others, like play dough, can be air-dried.

Make sure the clay or dough you are using is not too hard for little children to manipulate. Large pieces of clay are more difficult to handle and roll because of the size of a child's palms. A teaspoonful of clay is a good starting point for each child. How is a ball or sphere made? Place the clay in a palm and place the other palm on top. Then gently roll the clay between the palms. Try rubbing your palms from side to side, or up and down. What happens when you rub your palms in a clockwise motion? More clay or dough can be added as the balls take shape, if needed. Experiment with different amounts to make different sized balls.

These balls can be used to make beads. With adult help, a hole can be created in the centre of the sphere. Gently push a skewer into the centre of the ball through to the other side, before the clay dries. Remove the skewer carefully and leave the bead to dry. Use these unique beads to make simple jewellery.

Shopping for spheres

This idea came about when I was listening to Ryan playing in the garden. He had placed two chairs across the doorway to the toy shed and was shouting, 'Roll up, roll up. Come and get your balls from me! Best in the playground – roll up, roll up!' Within seconds he had a queue of children asking for a particular colour or type of ball to play with.

We hadn't been doing anything in particular about spheres at the time, but we had been encouraging children's skills in many areas of ball play: throwing and rolling for aim and speed. Ryan's technique for rousing support for ball games worked extremely well, with only two children continuing to play in the sandpit.

When we returned indoors, after the fun the children had had outside, Ryan suggested that we make a ball shop because everyone had liked his! After agreeing that, there had to be one rule – no throwing of balls indoors, the shop was planned.

> **TIP**
>
> Explain about the dangers of ball games indoors, especially when aiming is not always precise, tripping over balls left around, breaking of windows and objects, knocking over other children when running after balls, spoiling other activities, etc.

Once the corner was ready with a table (the counter), cash register and empty cardboard boxes to display the balls, we collected a few sponge balls, plastic holey balls, a plastic golf ball, tennis balls and a plastic football from the toy shed.

Back indoors, the shop was ready, and selling got under way immediately. To enable the children to use their purchases, we set aside an enclosed area for a skittle alley and a large mat where they could sit to roll balls to each other.

Once word spread to the parents about our ball shop, all sorts of sports' balls were brought in for display or to chat about during circle time.

The children were amazed by a set of boules brought in. They were similar to our set in the garden but, rather than being coloured plastic, these were much heavier, made of metal and very shiny with lines engraved around them.

We were able to display snooker balls and a triangular frame which we compared to a set of pool balls on loan. There were some brightly coloured golf balls and table tennis balls as well as a netball, cricket ball and a non-spherical leather rugby ball.

The balls were used for comparisons in size, weight, colour and texture. We talked about the different sports and, as there was so much interest, our next theme became sports!

The shop for selling balls was very successful indoors, with very few instances of a ball being thrown. Below are a couple of ideas when soft balls for indoor use come in very handy in our wet and windy climate.

Pass the soft ball

This is an excellent way of involving children in listening, concentrating, taking turns and speaking in a group situation.

The children sit in a circle facing the centre. A child is chosen to have the soft ball in their hand. Only the child holding the ball is allowed to speak; they may ask a question, tell an item of news, speak about an event or special happening, sing a song or describe something for others to guess at. Then they roll the ball to someone else who has raised their hand, to answer the question or guess the object or even carry on the conversation. Anyone who interrupts has to turn round with their back to the circle and miss one chance of a turn.

> **TIP** A sand timer can be used to limit the time any one child may speak about one thing.

Alternatively, the children sit as before in a circle. The child with the ball asks a child sitting either side to name their favourite colour. The ball is then rolled to a child wearing a piece of clothing of that colour. Play continues until everyone has had a turn rolling the ball or enough is enough!

Skittle alley

Before we had bought a set of plastic skittles, we made some. How this was done is described in Section 9: Cylinders.

Direction and speed of the ball are vital components when playing skittles. These are emergent skills in most three and four year olds. It takes a great deal of concentration, hand–eye co-ordination and strength to knock down several skittles. To experience the difficulty in this task, have a go yourself without using your preferred hand. Is it awkward or easy?

Our alley was a cardboard box from a washing machine. Use a craft knife to cut it in half, making two (one for later use). One side was cut down from two corners, leaving three sides attached to the base, and the fourth cut side made the alley base longer, ready for play.

> **TIP** The sides of the alley help to 'steer' wayward balls towards the skittles (on the rebound) so that children with little or no directional aim have a chance to knock one or two skittles down each time they roll (or throw) the balls.

Which marble makes it?

Our 'Which marble makes it maze' is based on the Labyrinth wooden puzzle game by House of Marbles®. During our theme on spheres, we borrowed this game for a short time, knowing it would need to be closely supervised because of the small marbles involved. It consists of a wooden box in which is balanced a wooden maze with holes along the marble's route. There are knobs on two sides of the box so that the maze can be tilted backwards and forwards and from side to side enabling the marble to move. The game requires a lot of concentration and well-developed hand–eye co-ordination skills to manoeuvre the marble from one end of the maze to the other without it falling through any of the holes. Once a marble has fallen through a hole, play passes to the next person.

Although the children enjoyed turning the knobs and tilting the board to manoeuvre a marble through the maze, the holes really got in their way in so many instances that the game became quite frustrating for them. Several of the children at our after-school club could manage the task but found it extremely disappointing to get almost to the end of the maze only to lose the marble down the last hole because their concentration went for a split second.

However, because the children obviously enjoyed the idea of negotiating through a maze and, rather than encountering a blocked path, liked the idea of a hole, Christine and I designed the 'Which marble makes it maze'. It can be played by a maximum of three children or used as an ordinary maze for one child to discover the way through. The black circles are the holes that can not be passed through or over.

Ingredients
A photocopy of the 'Which marble makes it maze' onto card and a marble or counter for each player.

Method
1. There are three starting points for the marbles. All start at the same entrance or each child starts at different entrances.
2. Turns are taken to move the marble through the maze. Whenever a hole is encountered, the marble is returned to the beginning again and the next player takes a new path to try their luck.
3. The first marble to remain on the path to the end wins.

We did stick a copy of the maze to a sheet of form board for durability because this game was a popular one to play. When asked by the children to make the holes 'real' we discovered that we didn't have any marbles small enough to go through the gaps!

The scope of our game was limited by A4 paper.

Blowing bubbles

How often do you do something on a regular basis and not 'see' beyond it? This happened to me twice during a topic on shape.

We were taking some balls out of the toy shed, when I suddenly noticed a missed opportunity to use our football in our shape theme. The pattern on the football was an ideal tessellation of hexagons and pentagons and no one had spotted it, even though the football was 'seen' almost every day.

The second time it happened just made me laugh.

The parents of a child who was leaving us to go to school had bought the nursery a battery-operated bubble gun as a gift. We opened it straight away and, once the machine was primed, bubbles streamed from the circular opening and, guess what, the bubbles were spherical.

I couldn't believe what I was seeing because only the fortnight before, a group of children and myself had been making different shaped wands to see if bubbles could be blown through them. We were talking about polygons (i.e. straight-sided shapes) and I had been so focused on that activity that I had missed the obvious outcome of blowing bubbles through an open ring!

What else have I missed over the years?

All the children in our pre-school love bubbles as much as I do, often asking challenging questions to see what we and bubbles are capable of.

- Do large bubbles travel further than tiny ones?
- How many bubbles can you catch on a wand before they pop?
- Is it best to blow hard to make big bubbles?
- Can you position a wand so that the breeze blows the bubbles for you?
- How long a trail of bubbles can you make?
- Have fun experimenting with straight-edged wands too.

Bubble painting

Ingredients
Sugar paper (A4 size for younger children), pots, circular lids, powder paint, brushes, washing up liquid, coloured straws.

> **TIP**   **Aprons must be worn as vigorous bubble blowing causes a lot of 'splash-back'.**

Method
1. Put equal amounts of water and washing up liquid into a pot before adding the paint. Mix together well. Add more paint to deepen the colour.
2. Pour the paint mixture into a flat-bottomed lid and blow bubbles into the paint with a straw.

> **TIP**
>
> Give children their favourite colour of straw to blow into, ensuring that they know how to blow – not suck. The straw can be used in any paint, but having their own means any germs are not spread.

3. Once bubbles start appearing, remove the straw and place a piece of paper over the bubbles and press gently.
4. Remove the paper and continue blowing and printing until painting is complete.

Section 8: Cube

	KUW	CLL	PSRN	C	P	PSE
70 What's special about a cube?	•	•	•			•
71 Creating crystals	•	•	•	•	•	
72 The dice of choice		•	•	•	•	•
73 Dice choices page					•	
74 Packing boxes	•	•	•	•		
75 Packing boxes page	•				•	
76 Construction site	•	•		•		•
77 Surprises come in small packages	•	•		•		•

A hexahedron is a polyhedron with six sides. Hexahedra are all three-dimensional solids and each side (face) has four edges. They have eight vertices (points or corners) and at each vertex three edges meet and include cuboids, rectangular prisms and cubes.

A cuboid is box-shaped and has six flat sides; all its internal angles are 90°. All of the sides are rectangles. It is also known as a rectangular prism.

If two opposite sides of the cuboid are squares, it can be called a square prism.

If all faces are squares, it is known as a cube. This solid is also a prism.

A cube is a special example of a square prism. A square prism is a special rectangular prism and they are all cuboids.

The name cuboid comes from 'cube' and 'oid' means resembling or similar to; so it is like a cube.

When we decided to 'do' cuboids as a theme in our pre-school, several children liked the idea of a cube collection. They wandered around the rooms in the nursery finding all they could to begin their quest.

A serious discussion took place between two boys who had found various bricks and disagreed whether a Lego® square brick could be included in their collection of cubes. 'It's not got six flat sides.' 'But it looks like a cube when it's in the wall.' We decided to resolve the dilemma during circle time when a vote was taken by all the children. The Lego® brick was discarded for having knobbly bits; the children followed the six flat sides rule!

Then a similar conversation took place over Unifix® cubes which a child had noticed in the collection. A couple of children objected to the description because they were not in fact cubes at all, with a raised top and a hole in it and no bottom at all! It definitely didn't have six flat sides of equal size. So they were discarded too. Our collection was dwindling by the minute.

However, the following day numerous Rubik's cubes were brought in for our collection: the early 1980s Rubik's cube craze. We even had a few edible exhibits; Oxo™ cubes in foil wrappers, white and brown sugar cubes and a plastic sweet jar filled with pineapple chunks from a sweet shop in town where they still sold sweets by weight. It stayed sealed and was the envy of our collection.

Added to the dice, threading cubes, wooden and plastic bricks of various sizes and cardboard boxes, our collection grew steadily.

Creating crystals

Way back in the 1970s when I first tried this experiment with children, growing crystals kits were not available as they are today, however the activity is still interesting and different. Nowadays, crystals have a wider influence and are used in various therapies. Different types of crystal may promote and enhance changes in emotions and in some instances allegedly have healing powers. In their natural state, crystals are found in all shapes and sizes. However, the crystals we grew formed into cubes.

Ingredients
Water, salt, jars or glasses, thread, pencil, small button, scissors, measuring cup and a tablespoon (or measuring spoon).

Method
1. Pour 150ml of water into a measuring cup and add four tablespoons of salt. Stir well, dissolving as much of the salt as possible.

> **TIP**
>
> Using hot water helps to speed up the process of dissolving the salt, but be aware of the dangers of using hot water around children.

2. Add one more tablespoon of salt. This salt solution is very strong and should not be drunk.
3. Thread the small button onto the thread and tie securely. Then tie the other end around a pencil so that when the pencil lies across the top of the jar, the button is about 2cm from the bottom of the jar or glass.
4. Fill the glass half full with the salt solution.
5. Place on a sunny windowsill or near a form of heat and leave undisturbed.
6. After 24 hours you may notice crystals forming on the thread, after two or three days remove the thread, and cubic crystals should have formed.

We enjoyed the experiment and decided to see what happens if the solution is disturbed several times as the crystals start to develop. Try it and discover for yourself.

What happens if a thick string is used instead of a thin thread?

Is there a difference in the crystals if nylon thread is used instead of cotton?

Would using wool make crystals of a different shape?

Does a button have to be added to the thread?

If the end of the thread is just touching the surface of the water rather than being in the solution, how does that affect the growing crystals?

Why not add food colouring to the salt solution to see what effect that has on the crystals. Try using less or more dye.

When some of the solution is poured into a saucer and allowed to evaporate, do crystals form? What shape are they? Use a magnifying glass to observe more closely.

Can sugar crystals be formed in the same way? Are they cubes?

The dice of choice

I remember a four-year-old suddenly giving a huge sigh and saying quite loudly, 'I'm so bored!' I was astounded. I asked Nicky why she was bored. Her reply was, 'There's nothing to do!'

I looked around the room and saw eight other children happily playing with a farmyard and road track, Duplo® and dressing up, another child engrossed in a puzzle and two children in the book corner talking about a book they were looking at. I quickly counted at least ten different activities in the room and said so to Nicky. Her retort was, 'But there's nothing I want to do!' and she wasn't very forthcoming as to what she *did* want to do. On going to the art room, her favourite place, there was nothing there she wanted to do either: only painting and chalking, sand and water and play-dough that session. She had really wanted to make something with cardboard.

Nicky attended nursery every day and, having experienced many of these activities before, I asked her if she would like to help me make something from cardboard. She would be able to use it whenever she felt there was nothing for her to do, and the dice of choice came into being.

Using the dice template in Part 2: Section 2, Nicky and I, together with a small group of other interested children, started to make several dice. On each flat side, before making up into a dice, the children chose six of the activities they liked to do best at nursery. We cut out pictures from educational catalogues and simple drawings to stick on each dice. Then, whenever the children were undecided what to do, they could throw their dice and the decision was made for them.

We used the same technique for outdoor play. Very often the balls or wheeled toys would be a chosen activity. With the dice being thrown, activities varied every session. We had one dice for the calm end of the garden and one dice for the more active games at the other end. The examples on the 'Dice choices page' for outdoor play are a mixture of the two but can be easily adapted to suit your setting.

The choice dice can be made for specific areas of learning too, e.g. mathematical, fine motor, gross motor and group game activities. We made dice for art and craft activities and another for imaginative play. The dice help rotate ideas so that different activities are available at different times. After all, variety is the spice of life!

Dice choices page

Packing boxes

We moved house several times while I was growing up and my brothers and sister loved playing in the empty tea chests that were used to pack away our breakables. The chests were about 18 inches square and probably a little deeper, so they weren't quite cubes. We often got splinters from the wooden sides but because they had metal edging, they made sturdy boxes for climbing on (when our parents weren't looking).

We each had one with our name written on the side so that we could pack away any toys that we wanted to take with us. Decisions on which toys would fit in the box while making sure it wasn't too heavy to lift, and how much space would be left for anything that could be squashed in at the end, were left to us children in the main. This got me thinking about fitting objects into boxes. If a toy was a wooden brick, it might be quite easy to guess which box it would fit in to. But what if the toy was an unusual shape, like a bicycle or ball? How big would the box have to be?

We collected a few cube-shaped boxes of different sizes. Then we gathered up a few toys from around the nursery to fit in the boxes. Which would go in where? It looked quite an easy game to play until we started. It was amazing how difficult some of the shapes were to gauge how wide, high or deep the box needed to be for the toy to fit. The smaller toys and objects fitted in most of the boxes, but awkward shapes were more puzzling and certainly more challenging.

We used tape measures, rulers and string to check widths and heights of items. Sometimes that helped, but if the shape was bumpy like a teddy bear, the measurements were often not too accurate and poor teddy might be squashed into too small a box. Often the children would just 'eye' the object up and estimate which box it would fit into, and this worked especially well with the balls for some reason. Probably a good thing too: measuring the width of a ball is challenging to say the least (unless you know the mathematical equation for working it out!).

Christine devised the 'Packing boxes page' to complement the game we had played with real boxes and toys. Photocopy the page and either measure the boxes and objects to see which will fit where, or make a slit in the top of each box, cut out the pictures and slot them into place.

Packing boxes page

Right from an early age, children love being able to knock over a tower of bricks. Then as they develop their manipulative skills further, a sense of frustration sets in when the tower keeps toppling over, since they want to make it as tall as it can be.

Maybe this is when they discover that by starting the base of their tower with two or four bricks, they can achieve a taller structure because they have begun with a stronger starting point. Later on, they will probably discover that by overlapping the base or first layer of bricks with a second row, they can increase the stability of their structure even more.

It happened with a child who was becoming very frustrated trying to build a barn for the cows in the farmyard. When he progressed to the third row of bricks, placing each one on top of the previous one, his walls kept collapsing. However, as he was picking up the bricks from his broken wall, he accidentally touched two bricks on the second layer so that they overlapped the first. When the bricks didn't fall, he turned to his friend to show him. 'Oh, that looks like a wall. What are you making? Can I help you?' They managed to build a wall of three bricks high using this 'new' technique.

As we were lucky enough to have some large plastic bricks that could be interlocked like a wall, we decided to have a construction site in the play corner. Hard hats from the dressing-up box, trowels, spades and buckets from the sand tray, some assorted bricks, and our building site was ready. However, our group of builders soon let us know that there was something missing. Cups of tea and cans of coke are a must on any building site apparently!

Junk modelling

The building site spilt over into the art room. All shapes and sizes of boxes, cubes and cuboids, were used in making some incredible structures, several of which were as high as the tallest children.

> **TIP** Use masking tape to 'stick' boxes together. There is no need for scissors as it is easy for children to tear and can be painted afterwards.

Most of the models were painted in a variety of colours, but one or two children made their structure into something specific. An attic room with windows in the roof was the reason behind the house with windows painted on every visible surface. It also had a front door and French patio doors at the back. Another had windows all over; it was an office block in Leicester where Sophie's dad worked.

Surprises come in small packages

Following on from the previous activity, one small cubed box had been painted in thin stripes. When we mentioned to Jonathan how carefully he had painted his box, he said it was because it was a surprise box. At the end of the day, when the box was dry, Jonathan picked it up to take home and it rattled. He grinned at us and said, 'That's the surprise, there's something hiding inside. Guess what it could be?'

Jonathan would not give us a clue and thought it great fun to tease us and his friends. Then Dean suggested that he hold the box to see if he could 'feel' what it was inside the box. Almost as soon as Jonathan handed it over, Dean said, 'It's a car!' He was right, it was possible to 'feel' the movement and weight and hear the sound it made on the box's sides. Jonathan had brought the car from home and had thought it would be a safe place to put it while he painted his box and it would be a surprise when the box was opened!

That was how our next activity came to be.

Ingredients
Several different sizes of boxes, objects of various weights and sizes, and pieces of masking tape.

Method
1. Fit an object into a box so that there is some room for movement.
2. Close the top of each box with a small strip of masking tape, ensuring the contents can not be seen.
3. Take turns to pick up a box and guess its contents by weight, size, movement and sound.

> **TIP**
> Depending on the number of boxes used in the activity, change the objects in some of the boxes after two or three have been guessed correctly. Regular swapping will ensure that there are always new 'surprises' in the boxes.

To make the activity and identification of objects easier, allow the children to see the objects before they are placed in the individual boxes.

We also used this idea during circle time, when we would place an unseen object into a box and give one clue as to the contents. Sometimes the clue would have a very obvious answer, whereas on other occasions several clues needed to be given to find the surprise.

The surprise box can be used during any theme you have in your setting. The surprise box also enhanced some story and rhyme times. Put an object related to your chosen story into the box, give clues as to the contents and, when the object is guessed at, which story or rhyme could it belong to?

Section 9: Cylinder

	KUW	CLL	PSRN	C	P	PSE
78 What's special about a cylinder?	•	•	•	•	•	•
79 Sound cylinders	•	•		•	•	•
80 Textured tubes		•		•	•	
81 Our skittle alley	•	•	•	•	•	•
82 The tube family page		•				
83 Our tube family	•	•	•			•
84 Fitting in – a square peg in a round hole		•	•	•		•
85 Fitting in shapes page			•		•	

A cylinder is a solid figure. It is three-dimensional having two parallel flat sides and a closed curved surface. The parallel flat sides are always circles.

When the children suggested a cylinder collection, like we had made with cubes, I thought there would be few items that would fit the bill.

However, it was soon after Christmas when we began the theme of cylinders, and cylindrical sweet containers were brought in by the bagful; all empty of course. We also had a selection of larger cylinders that had contained savoury morsels.

Around the nursery we found lengths of plastic tubing from the water toys, straws, paint rollers, pieces of dowelling and wooden bricks.

There were numerous examples of cardboard tubes in our recycling box, including carpet rolls, tubes for mailing posters, wrapping paper inner tubes and kitchen roll inners.

Our collection grew at an alarming rate. Parents brought in cylindrical biscuit tins, candles, wide wooden bangles, drinks cans (without the contents) and even a mug without a handle.

On a walk to the park we noticed many other cylindrical objects. The 'lollipop' lady, whose sign we had already noted as circular, had a cylindrical stick to hold up her sign. The telegraph poles were enormously tall and not one child could reach all the way round. Some of the litter bins were attached to poles in the ground and all these poles were cylindrical.

Take a walk to your local park or playground and see how many cylinders you spot.

An outing to the supermarket was a real eye-opener: hundreds of cylindrical items on nearly every shelf!

The children were intrigued by the number of different tubes in the recycling box. So we tipped out the contents of the box into an empty (and dry) water tray. The children sorted out all the cylinders, and everything else was returned to the box.

Kyle and Joshua sorted the tubes further, first by length and then by diameter. They began to arrange these tubes in order, starting with the inner from a roll of sticky tape. Then they picked a tube that would fit inside this shallow, but wide, cylinder. They continued, repeatedly finding narrower and narrower tubes. After several minutes they had inadvertently made a set of nesting cylinders of which they were very proud. They both wanted to take the tube nest home. So we used a craft knife to cut the tubes in half, except for the sticky tape inner which was too narrow. However, Kyle found another in the tray and so both boys went home happy!

Sound cylinders

The empty sweet tubes that were brought in for our cylinder collection came in very handy for another purpose. They were all the same size and had removable lids and fixed bases. The only differences between them were the pictures around the curved sides, and for this activity that was not a problem. However, you could easily cover each tube with white or coloured paper to hide the pictures if you prefer.

We made some sound-matching cylinders. The idea of the game was to encourage and develop children's listening and auditory discrimination skills. Pairs of tubes had different items put into them. Then one tube was shaken or moved gently and its matching 'sound twin' had to be found among the other tubes.

Ingredients
Tubes with bases and lids, dried beans, rice, feathers or two small balls of wool, paper clips, sand, sequins or small beads, plastic straws or any other small objects that make a sound in the tube, sticky tape and scissors.

Method
1. Choose pairs of tubes with pictures that do not match.

> **TIP**
> If the pairs of tubes match, then children will quickly realise that they do not need to listen carefully to spot the sounds, but just match the sweet pictures instead.

2. Put equal amounts of dried peas or beans in one pair of tubes. Close the lid and check they both sound the same before securing the lid with sticky tape. Adjust the amounts if necessary to ensure the sounds are identical.
3. Fill the other pairs of tubes in a similar way until there are several sounds to listen out for. Vary the contents to make different pitches and tones when the tubes are moved.

> **TIP**
> Be aware that some of the contents may weigh heavier than others. If the activity is being used without adult supervision and guidance, then children may match by weight rather than sound.

4. A child may shake, roll or gently tilt a tube for their friend to find a matching sound in another tube, or use as a group activity.

Try the same activity using larger savoury containers that have metal bases and plastic lids for different sound-making games. Experiment with similar contents and amounts and notice whether the pitch and tone changes with the change of cylinder size or base.

Use these tubes with lids for the children to develop their fine manipulative skills by filling up the cylinders and pouring out the contents back into their original container. They are an added attraction to any dry sand activity too!

Textured tubes

Nowadays, in educational catalogues, pieces of equipment that can be used for printing are ten a penny. There are plastic blocks with handles, and paint rollers which have patterns and textures on them for repeated printing and pattern making. They are well made and last for years, I'm sure. However, before these were developed commercially, we had to make our own.

I feel fairly confident to say that most early years' practitioners will have made some kind of printing block; most probably with potatoes, corks or string glued to a piece of wood. Paint rollers could be bought from most hardware stores but were difficult to clean and re-use after having powder or poster paints on them. They were not particularly long lasting either because the foam broke off or the fleece became very ragged. We often made our own textured rollers using tubes and pencils or rolling pins (usually used for play-dough and clay activities).

We would collect samples of textured wallpaper from a DIY shop or ask parents for off-cuts that they would normally have thrown away, to make a variety of rollers.

Ingredients
Hollow tubes, pieces of textured wallpaper, PVA glue, glue brushes or spatulas, scissors, rolling pins (small enough to fit into the tubes), painting paper, paints, brushes and aprons.

Method
1. Ensure that each child is suitably protected with an apron.
2. Spread glue thoroughly over the whole tube.
3. Place the textured paper smooth side uppermost on a flat surface and roll the tube over it, making sure it is stuck down firmly.
4. Leave to dry.

> **TIP**
>
> The rollers work best if left overnight so that the cardboard tube is thoroughly dry before paint is added to the outer wallpaper.

5. Cover the tube with paint using a brush.
6. Place the rolling pin inside the tube and push the roller over paper to make a textured pattern.

The children can mix and match patterns and colours until they are happy with the picture they have created.

Try using pieces of dowelling or thicker cardboard tubes for longer lasting rollers.

Wrapping wool, string or raffia around the tubes will create more textures. These threads can be glued in place or, attaching one end of the string inside the tube with sticky tape, wrap the string around and then fasten it inside the tube securely.

When using dowelling, leave the ends free of paper or thread so that it can be handled and rolled without getting too much paint on little fingers.

In the previous section on cubes, I mentioned that we made skittles from various cylinders which we used in our skittle alley.

They are very quick and simple to make and if you have tubes with bases and lids, the task is even quicker.

When we first used cardboard cylinders in this way, we had only the inner tubes from kitchen paper rolls. Without any modifications at all, they worked well indoors with soft balls. However, outdoors any small breeze or little gust of wind will topple them without the need for any balls at all. We decided the skittles needed a more stable base.

We fixed circular bases to each skittle and poured a tablespoonful of sand into the bottom. Before adding a top (to keep the sand from spilling out) we checked that the skittles were more stable and that they could be toppled fairly easily. Add more sand if necessary and then secure the top with another circle of card.

The children really liked the idea of the skittles and, as they were so simple to make, we asked parents to collect tubes from food covering, aluminium foil and kitchen paper so that each child could make a small set of skittles.

Some of the tubes were cut in half and children played with them instantly, while others decided to paint or decorate their skittles before using them. Several tubes were so small in diameter that ordinary balls were too big to play skittles with. We found table tennis balls adequate to knock a couple of skittles down, but marbles worked brilliantly. Many of the cut-down tubes required no sand, but some of the thinner tubes needed a little to help make them more stable, especially if used outdoors.

We experimented with and chatted about the different types of cylindrical containers to find which made a good skittle.

- Is it possible to knock down a ten-centimetre diameter cylinder with a sponge ball?
- Which skittles can be toppled with only an ordinary marble?
- How far away from the skittles do you have to be to knock them all down?
- What happens if you put balls of newspaper into the tubes instead of sand?

Most children thought the best skittles were ones they could knock down easily or the ones they had made! But there was a unanimous decision as to the worst type of skittle: one that toppled as soon as it was set up, and even our shop-bought ones did that occasionally!

The tube family page

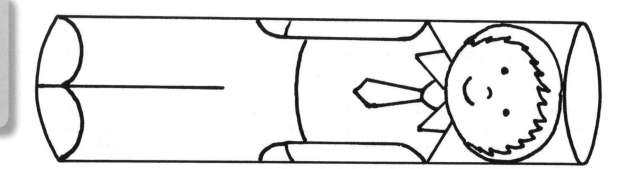

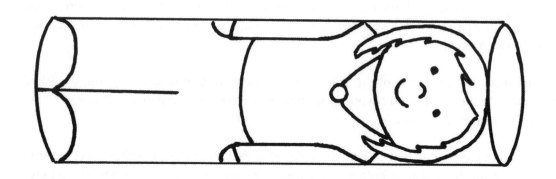

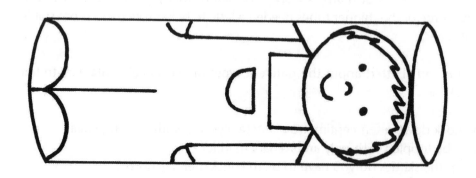

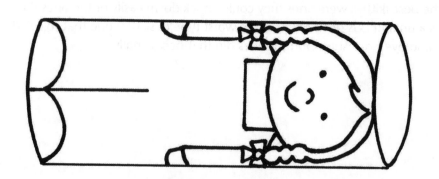

Our tube family

In the previous activity when the children were decorating their skittles, Christine decided she would make a skittle family. She chose tubes of slightly different heights and, without telling the children what she intended to do, started painting their shoes. As she began painting the trousers on the 'dad', Emily asked her what she was doing and was quite horrified to think that 'people' were going to be skittles. 'Can't they just be a family that doesn't get knocked over?'

The consensus of opinion around the art table was that the tube family would not become skittles. As Christine carried on painting trousers on the 'mum', the children asked lots of questions about why was the daddy the tallest? What colour trousers is the little girl going to have? What are their names? How old is the boy? Christine began to tell the life story of each member of the family, answering the children's questions as she went.

The little group of tubes became known as the Tube family; Toby was the son, Tinks was the daughter and mum and dad were Mr and Mrs Tube, Tim and Tina. They were kept in a box which eventually had a gramps and granny and a dog and cat added.

The Tubes were a popular storytime addition and went on many adventures, often to places beginning with 'T'. They drove tanks in Turkey and trekked across Tasmania, always stopping at Tesco® for their provisions.

However, dad was always wearing a collar and tie in our original image, so Christine made another 'dad' to glue to the other side of the tube so that he looked more casual when trekking across countries or driving a tank.

Use the images on 'The tube family page' to create your own family for story time, imaginative play activities and, dare I suggest, skittles!

Whether the images are left as they are or enlarged so that they fit around the front of different sized tubes, cut each member of the family out. Before sticking to the tubes, crayon each picture to add colour to their clothes and make them more individual.

The people have been drawn with simple lines so that you can develop your own tube people. Add a stethoscope around Mrs Tube's neck instead of a necklace and she becomes Dr Tube. With the addition of a hat and sparkly sequins, Mr Tube could become a Wizard Tube.

With a little imagination, paint and a brush, tubes can become almost any character in a story. Glue or tape a lollipop stick to the inside of the tube and the character becomes a puppet to enact the story.

Fitting in – a square peg in a round hole

After watching a couple of children trying to master a posting shapes ball, I remembered this phrase and an incident that happened when I was about seven years old as the basis for the next activity.

A friend at school told me his dad thought he was a round peg in a square hole because he wanted to be a dancer. Neither of us knew what the phrase meant, except that Peter was not going to join his sister at her dancing classes. When I got home from school I asked my mum what a round peg in a square hole meant.

The saying that she knew was a square peg in a round hole and it meant 'something that did not fit'. She asked why I needed to know, so after explaining about Peter, she replied that the phrase usually applied to a person who was not suited to a job or task, someone who did not fit in or would be out of place.

It was the early 1960s and long before *Billy Elliot*, but I had been to the theatre to see ballets with my parents and knew that boys danced, so Peter wouldn't be out of place or not fit in. He loved Scottish country dancing classes at school, so I knew he would be suited to it. I had difficulty understanding why Peter would be a square peg. My mum explained that although what I said was true, many parents would prefer their boys to take up football. I played cricket with my brothers and, although I was the only girl, I had never been told I was a round peg in a square hole or that I had to do 'girlie' things.

The idea of equality of opportunity for all has stayed with me since that day and has ensured that during my work with children I have sincerely tried to be true to that philosophy.

Fitting in shapes game

Photocopy the 'Fitting in shapes page' onto card and cut out each individual shape. Make slits in the cylinder tops. Compare each shape with the top of the narrowest. How many shapes fit in? Which shapes fit in more than one tube?

If the shapes are not cut out, how can you decide which fits where? What sort of measuring devices can you use?

To enhance the difficulty of the activity, re-draw the square as a rectangle, the rectangle as a square; can they fit in more tubes now?

Cut out polygon images from other activity pages to try, or use 'real' cylinders and solids to make your own posting shapes game.

Section 10: Pyramid and cone

	KUW	CLL	PSRN	C	P	PSE
86 What's special about a pyramid?	•	•	•		•	
87 Pyramid templates page					•	
88 The camel race	•	•	•	•	•	•
89 Camel race page		•				
90 What's special about a cone?	•	•	•			
91 Cones come alive		•	•	•	•	•
92 Conical figures				•		
93 Ice cream parlour	•	•	•	•	•	•

A pyramid is a polyhedron: a solid three-dimensional object where the base is a polygon, i.e. a straight-sided shape. The sides are triangles which meet at the top, or apex.

Pyramids are always named after the shape of their bases. So a pyramid with a triangular base is called a triangular pyramid, and a square pyramid will have a square base.

The great pyramids of Egypt are square pyramids and can be made quite simply by using the template on the 'Pyramid templates page'. Your pyramids can enhance the camel race game as three-dimensional visual effects.

To make an Egyptian pyramid

Ingredients
A photocopy of the 'Pyramid templates page' onto card, scissors, glue or masking tape and a ruler.

> **TIP**   Enlarge the image if required to make a selection of different sized square pyramids. If a rigid structure is required, try out different papers and cards to prevent the sides and base of larger pyramids from becoming too floppy.

Method
1. Cut out around the outline.
2. Score along each line using the ruler to ensure straight lines.
3. Fold along each line to make up the solid.
4. Secure the flaps inside or outside the pyramid with glue or masking tape.
5. Decorate with Egyptian symbols or paint once the glue has dried.

Examples of 'stepped' square pyramids can be made using virtually any bricks.

To show children how to make a simple stepped square pyramid, begin with nine cubed bricks arranged into a square, i.e. three bricks in each row. Then add four cubes, arranged centrally, on top of the first step, with a final cube on the top.

Most bricks make very good square stepped pyramids but, if they are not connected, can easily lose their shape if knocked. The idea can be developed further depending on each child's fine manipulative skills and hand–eye co-ordination.

Duplo® and Lego® bricks are ideal for making a more permanent structure as they can link together and retain their shape.

We experimented with a photocopied page of squares (from Section 4: Square) glued to a piece of corrugated cardboard. Once dry, we carefully cut out each square and placed them on top of each other in size order. Once centralised, they made an excellent stepped pyramid which many children had a go at making when the pieces were left unstuck.

What's special about a pyramid?

> **TIP**
> This works extremely well with a sheet of form board, being more durable than corrugated cardboard.

The other template on the 'Pyramid templates page' makes a triangular pyramid. We made several as four-sided dice for games and making choices (as mentioned in previous activities).

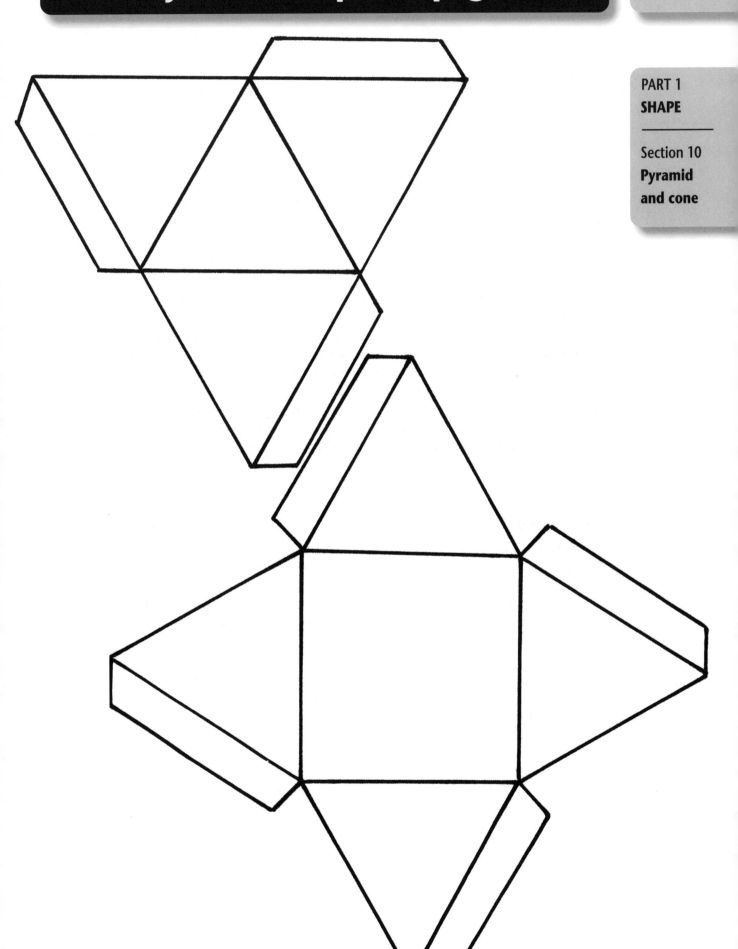

The camel race

The camel race game started life in our playground during a theme on visiting famous places in the world. We were in 'Egypt', surrounded by several pyramids made from large cardboard boxes that we had placed around the garden. We were on 'guided tours' learning about Tutankhamen, the pharaohs, the Sphinx and pyramids, when Christine and I decided to turn the tour into a game.

We drew chalk circles on the tarmac around the pyramids and decided that to travel by camel was by far the most sensible mode of transport to get us to the oasis at the end of the track. The game worked well, taking turns to throw the dice and move around Egypt and the pyramids.

However, the children decided that a little danger along the way was called for and ran indoors to collect some 'hazards'. They came back with a selection of plastic lizards and snakes which they placed at various points along the track. The children decided that the lizards were really scorpions which would sting if you landed on them, meaning a turn was missed. A snake in your path would make you back away – two spaces. The children felt that the game was much more exciting with these added extras. It certainly took longer to reach the oasis but the children thoroughly enjoyed the adventure. Not quite Indiana Jones but close!

Christine adapted these ideas to make our board game, which was originally drawn on a piece of A3 card. Initially we used coloured counters for each participant playing the game, but later on we made stand-up figures of camels (in different colours) which the children moved along the camel footprints.

The board game

Photocopy the 'Camel race page' onto card, enlarging if necessary. Because this game was very popular, we coloured in the images on the board and laminated it so that it would last longer.

Our rules were similar to the game we played outside but, with the addition of the double foot-prints, shortcuts could be taken. However, discuss with your group the types of rules they want. Below are a few questions which might help to get your rules started.

- How will the game start? Is a 6 needed or someone whose name begins with . . . ?
- Do you return to the beginning if you land on a snake?
- What happens if a scorpion stings you?
- Can two camels be on the same footprint at the same time?
- Will you miss a turn or go back a space if you throw a 1?

Be aware that rules have consequences, making the game over too quickly, repetitive or even tedious to play. Be prepared to change!

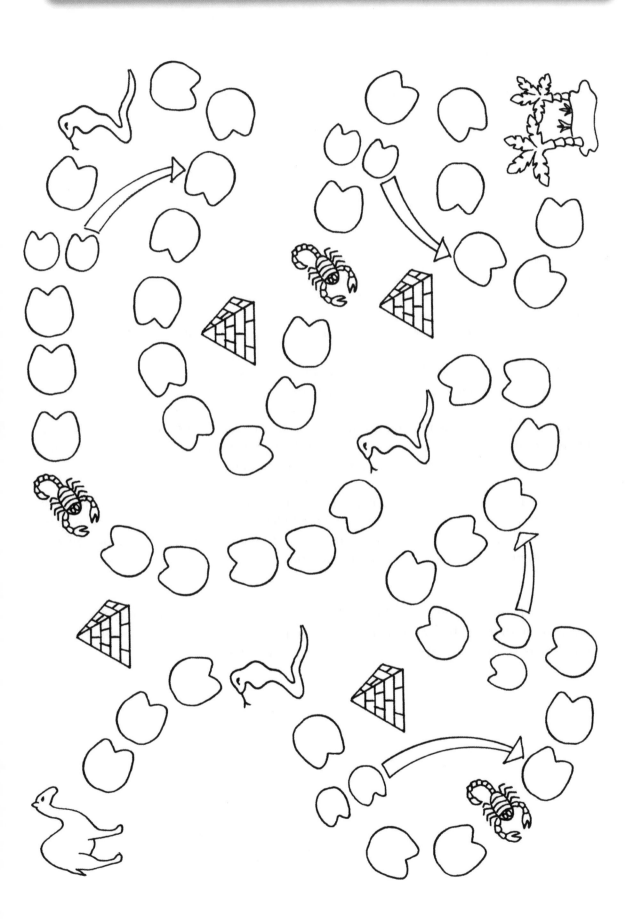

What's special about a cone?

A cone is a three-dimensional object that has a circular base which is a flat surface.

Cones are interesting because they have only one curved side which tapers up to an apex.

A cone is not a polyhedron, nor is it a prism because it has a curved surface.

The children were very interested in the shape of a cone because it reminded them of ice creams and they decided that a table of cones would be a good idea. I must admit, I wasn't so sure. I found it difficult to think of many things that were cone shaped apart from the obvious ice-cream cone.

However, by the end of the week we had a couple of traffic cones on our display table. One was small and green and had been borrowed from the Scouts; the other was from an unknown source but had been found in a front garden just off the main road (near to some road works!). Joseph proudly marched into nursery one afternoon with three miniature traffic cones from his road mat set, 'You can borrow these for a couple of days, if you look after them!'

We also had a red, white and blue cone advertising a local fish and chip restaurant and a similar cone with pictures of chips all over it from a shop in another town.

Our play-food box was raided to find a couple of plastic ice cream cones we had in there. The children decided only the cones were allowed on their display and so the ice-cream scoops attached by pieces of Velcro® were pulled off and returned to the food box.

A mum, who did a lot of machine knitting, also provided us with some cones from the inside of her wool cones. One or two were made of coloured plastic but the majority were made from cardboard. She said we were welcome to use them for junk modelling once the display was finished. They were put to good use during the following week for some of the following activities!

One thing we hadn't envisaged when embarking on this theme was the amount and variety of cones we received through word of mouth; however, perhaps we should have stressed that the cones we were collecting were geometric solids, not from fir trees!

The knitting wool cones from the previous collection gave us the idea for this activity.

Years ago I had read a children's craft book which showed how to make pop-up puppets using cones like these. However, whenever we had made the puppets with children, the activity was heavily reliant on an adult, and most children under five needed a great deal of help. So Christine and I have simplified the idea so that if knitting cones are not available, almost any child can make a puppet without a lot of adult input.

This is also a lovely activity for children who are good at cutting out to share with someone less adept. The puppets can be any size depending on the circle template used. For example – if drawing around a cup, the cone will be tiny, but using a dinner plate will produce a much taller cone.

Cone puppets

Ingredients
Thick paper or card, scissors, pencils and crayons, masking tape or glue, circular templates, fabric scraps, collage materials and thread or wool.

Method
1. Draw around the template as accurately as possible.
2. Cut around the outline and then fold the circle in half. Cut along the fold to make two semi-circles.
3. Wrap a straight edge over the other straight edge to make a cone shape. Secure with glue or masking tape.
4. Flatten the cone and draw features on one or both sides to make a person or creature.

Our 'Conical figures' page offers some examples of how to make a cone come to life.

Add fabric to give a person a cloak or dress, wool makes excellent hair, tails or whiskers, paper scraps can become ears, legs or tails. Attach string or wool to the inside bottom edge of the cone to make a pair of legs, add little paper shoes or fabric for trousers.

We also attached thread to the apex of the cones so that some of the characters could hang from window frames and swing round. This idea came in handy at Christmas when we made angels with wings. Use green card and stick on sequins as baubles for Christmas tree cones.

We painted some of the knitting wool cones in bright colours and then, starting at the top, wrapped metallic ribbon around them, attaching it inside the cone at the bottom. They were hung from the trees outside and twirled around in the smallest of breezes. We threaded some large metallic-shaped sequins to the bottom edges too and, when the sun caught them as they twirled, they cast lovely reflections on the walls and ground.

Try hanging other things from these heavier cones to make wind chimes.

Conical figures

We had real fun when we made an ice cream stall following on from the idea of making cones.

The stall

Ingredients
Table, mailing tubes or similar, paints, coloured paper, glue and masking tape.

Method
1. Paint or wrap the tubes so they are colourful.
2. Attach the tubes to each leg of the table with masking tape.
3. Cut long strips of paper and fix them to the top of the upright poles to suggest the roof of the stall.
4. Add a name to the stall, if necessary.

The ice creams

Ingredients
Quarter-circles of brown sugar paper or similar (8cm or more radius), brown or black crayons, glue, cotton wool, tissue paper, plastic containers (for ice cream), scoops or spoons and menu board.

Method
1. Draw chequered patterns on the quarter-circles of paper to resemble the wafer cones, and make them as described in the previous activity.
2. Screw up different colours of tissue paper corresponding to flavours of ice creams, or use cotton wool rolled into balls, as individual scoops of ice cream. Place the different 'flavours' of ice cream into different containers ready for sale.

> **TIP**
>
> Buying coloured cotton wool balls saves time, however, the colours are often limited but, given their imagination, the children's play will not be.

3. Make a menu board with the flavours of ice cream depicted by colour, as well as with writing, and attach it to the stall.
4. Use the scoops or spoons to put the ice cream into the cones as they are purchased.

This is an effective play corner and was very popular whenever we had a holiday or seaside theme, a carnival play area, a circus or just a stand-alone activity.

When we used coloured cotton wool balls, the children were very inventive with the flavours. The vanilla (white) was also rice pudding or additive-free ice cream. The pale yellow cotton wool was banana, lemon and butterscotch ice cream as well as lemon sorbet. Strawberry was, of course, pink, and nothing rivalled that! However, one little girl decided to have two scoops: one rhubarb, the other custard – guess their colours? The pale blue cotton wool balls were initially discarded until someone decided that sea fresh ice cream sounded, and probably, tasted good and was added to our menu!

The idea can be extended to an ice cream parlour with chairs and tables, waiters or waitresses, kitchen, etc. just like a small café, or as an ice cream van waiting outside a school or shopping area for customers.

Part 2: Colour

Section 1: Activities for all

	KUW	CLL	PSRN	C	P	PSE
94 Making rainbows	•	•	•	•	•	•
95 Singing a rainbow	•	•		•		
96 Rainbow mobile			•	•	•	
97 Rainbow mobile puzzle activity page					•	
98 Rainbow puzzle			•	•	•	
99 Going for gold game	•	•	•	•	•	•
100 Colourful scene	•	•	•	•	•	•
101 Park scene page		•				
102 Colour rhymes		•				
103 Colour rhymes activity page	•	•				
104 Games		•	•	•		•
105 Games page					•	
106 Colour games	•	•	•	•		
107 Spinning wheels page					•	
108 Spinning colours	•		•	•	•	
109 Colourful displays			•	•		•

Making rainbows

Rainbows have fascinated me since I was a very young child. I always wanted the sun to come out whenever it was raining because I knew I might be able to spot a rainbow, especially if I had my back to the sun while it carried on raining.

A rainbow happens when rays of sunlight enter raindrops and are refracted, or bent. Some of the refracted light then reflects from the interior of each water droplet, which splits the rays of white light into their constituent colours of the spectrum, or rainbow. The red colour is always at the top of the rainbow.

A double rainbow occurs when the raindrops reflect light twice. The higher rainbow reverses the colours of the lower one, with violet at the top.

There are several ways a rainbow effect can be made with very little preparation or props – but sunlight comes in very handy.

Fill a glass with water and put it on a windowsill in direct sunlight. Where the sun passes through the glass of water, look for a rainbow on the wall or floor in the room.

Alternatively, if it is a cloudy day, use a glass of water, a mirror and a torch to achieve a similar effect. Go into a dark room or try with a dark cardboard box. Put a mirror at an angle in a glass of water. Shine a bright torch onto the mirror and look around for the rainbow. Move the mirror in the glass if need be to see the rainbow more clearly. Try using different torches for unusual effects – different types of torchlight refract through the water differently.

Hold or hang a clear crystal (or glass bauble) in sunlight to see rainbows around your room. If you spin the crystal while hanging from a thread, the rainbows will flicker about the walls or floor for lovely colourful effects.

On a sunny day in your outside play area, use a watering can fitted with a fine rose to make rainbows. When the water is poured through the holes in the path of direct sunlight, a rainbow will appear through the spray. This also works extremely well with an adjustable nozzle attachment on a hose or by walking around a garden sprinkler. A rainbow will be seen by looking into the mist that is produced.

Don't forget – look for the pot of gold at the end of the rainbow!

Singing a rainbow

When I was at primary school I can remember being taught a mnemonic for the colours of the rainbow. A mnemonic is a system to help and improve memory. The word comes from the Greek 'to remember' and was personified in Greek mythology as Mnemosyne, the daughter of Uranus and the mother of the Muses, the goddesses of poetry and literature. The rainbow mnemonic saying was 'Richard of York gave battle in vain'. The initial letter of each word corresponds to the initial letters of the colours in a rainbow, starting at the top: red, orange, yellow, green, blue, indigo and violet.

I didn't know it was called a mnemonic until many years later when a friend came to visit. I was looking after some gerbils during the school holidays and my friend mentioned that gerbils always reminded her of a mnemonic to do with rainbows. I understood the term once she said, 'Run over your gerbil because it's vicious – you know red, orange, yellow, green, blue, indigo, violet.' I had never heard the saying before and it is perhaps one not to mention to your early years' group!

My friend wondered why we had learnt the colours of a rainbow in order like that when the 'I can sing a rainbow' song is so well known. I mentioned that a teacher at school had said the rainbow song was incorrect, with the wrong colours and sung in the wrong order and that was why she had taught us the saying. As my friend started to sing the song, she was so surprised because she hadn't really listened to the words before.

In all the early years' settings where I have worked, the children have sung 'I can sing a rainbow' without anyone explaining the inconsistencies. It has always unsettled me. I like to mention the 'real' colours, preferably in the correct order, whenever I use the song in activities or during circle time.

There is a school musical called 'Noah and the Rainbow Ark', where God puts a rainbow in the sky, making the world beautiful again after the flood. The rainbow song is very catchy, the colours are sung in the correct order but, unfortunately, the lyrics are under licence and have to be bought.

However, all is not lost because children love rhyming games, and if you use simple rhymes as a starting point, you'll have a whole lot of fun!

> Roses are red, in the garden they grew
> Oranges are orange, with dimples too.
> Buttercups are yellow, grass is green,
> Blues in the sky are often seen.
> Indigo is dark blue, very deep.
> Violet's like purple, oh, so sweet. (poetic licence!)

Rainbow mobile

The 'Rainbow mobile puzzle activity page' is useful for a number of activities.

Mobile

Ingredients

A photocopy of the page stuck onto card for each child, scissors, crayons, hole punch, needle and thread, masking tape is optional.

Method

1. Colour in the rainbow, flowers, cloud and sunshine.
2. Cut out each image as carefully as possible. The flowers do not need to be cut out separately. Certain children may need help cutting out the rainbow, as the stripes are long. The children may find cutting at an angle difficult as the stripe next to each one is not discarded but needed for the mobile.

> **TIP**
> If you are required to cut out several rainbows, place the sheets together so that the rainbow outlines line up with each other, staple the pages together (avoiding the other images) so that several rainbows can be cut out while only cutting out one.

3. Punch a hole towards the top and bottom of the cloud and sun.
4. Punch a hole near to the centre of each section of the rainbow.
5. Punch a hole towards the top of the group of flowers.
6. Thread a blunt needle with the yarn and begin putting together the mobile.
7. The sun can be positioned above the cloud or vice versa – it depends entirely upon each individual child. They may like the sun to shine down through the rain, or they may prefer the rain to filter through the sun's rays.
8. Secure each piece with a loose knot.

> **TIP**
> Masking tape on the reverse of each section will stop them from sliding into each other if preferred. Masking tape is less sticky than ordinary tape and can also be crayoned over, if necessary.

9. The positioning of the rainbow strips is important and your newly made up mnemonics (singing a rainbow) may help put them in order.
10. The flowers are the last to be threaded – without the sun and rain they would not grow!

Making this mobile takes a great deal of concentration, hand–eye co-ordination, determination and perseverance. At one setting where I worked, younger children who wanted a go completed the activity in stages. One child with special needs, who wanted to take part, spent time every day during one week adding 'bits' to her rainbow. We enlarged each section so that she could see more clearly and helped her with cutting and threading. She loved the rainbow so much that she decided to paint the reverse of each section – to hide the tape, she said! How fortunate that our setting was prepared and able to accommodate individuals in this way.

Rainbow puzzle

Another way of utilising the 'Rainbow mobile puzzle activity page' is to make a puzzle that can double up as a game.

Puzzle

Ingredients
Photocopy of the page onto card for durability, pencil or pen and scissors. Crayons or felt pens are optional.

Method
1. For an extremely simple puzzle, draw a wavy line across the middle of the page and then cut along the line to make two pieces.
2. These two pieces can then be cut again, making four. That may be difficult enough for some children to deal with, for others six, eight or more pieces may be required.

> **TIP**
> The difficulty increases if the line is cut from corner to corner.

Using the black and white image can make for a difficult puzzle without too many pieces being involved. Try it yourself and see before cutting the picture into twelve pieces! Add a bit of colour to just the rainbow and notice the difference in difficulty.

Colour the whole picture before cutting. This will give children an extra 'clue' to matching each piece together, like in a real puzzle.

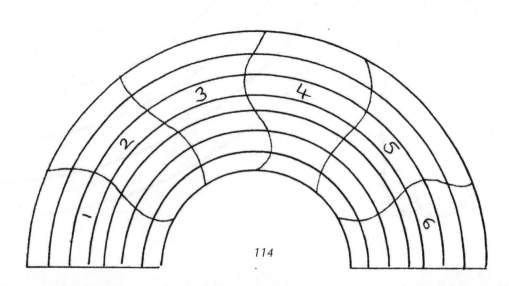

This game is based on the idea that there is a pot of gold at the end of every rainbow. To get there you need to collect the pieces of the rainbow in order.

There is a little preparation (for the early years' practitioner) to do before starting this game with a group of children. Only the rainbow and the sun images are required from the 'Rainbow mobile puzzle activity page' for this game. You may want to reduce them so that two games can be made from one A4 sheet of card.

Ingredients
One photocopy onto card of the rainbow and the sun is required for each child participating in the game, an ordinary dice, coloured crayons, gold paint and brushes or gold crayons, ribbon or yarn, sticky tape and scissors.

Method
1. Cut out and paint or colour the sun gold. When it is dry, add the ribbon or yarn to make a gold medal – the pot of gold.
2. Colour the rainbow in appropriate colours and cut out.
3. Divide the rainbow into six sections along its length, numbering each piece from 1 on the left-hand side to 6 at the other end.
4. Cut the numbered sections and the game is ready.

How to play
1. Each player takes turns to throw the dice.
2. The rainbow is made in numerical order. A '1' needs to be thrown before a rainbow can be started. Then a 2 and so on.
3. Once a 6 is thrown to complete the rainbow, the child is awarded the golden sun medal to signify reaching the pot of gold at the end of the rainbow.
4. The game can end there or, as happens on most occasions, everyone taking part wants to reach the end of the rainbow for their 'pot of gold'.

It is amazing how popular this game is with the children. They enjoy wearing a gold medal at the end and didn't mind the, often, long wait to throw the correct number each time because the 'pot of gold' at the end was well worth the wait!

Any game played with a group of children will help to develop many skills within the Early Years Foundation Stage.

PSE – patience, tolerance and concentration required while waiting turns.
KUW – following rules supports the idea that actions have consequences.
PSRN – understanding the relationship between patterns (on a dice) and numerals is an important skill in mathematical development.
P – using counters, dice and cards boosts fine motor skills and improves manual dexterity.
CLL / C – interaction between players encourages imaginative and creative thinking skills.

The 'Park scene page' is full of objects that can be many different colours. When I first looked at the picture I saw the slide as red and yellow like the one in our playground – it even had the same number of rungs on the ladder. The bucket was silver, why I don't know – we had no metallic buckets in our sand tray. I wondered if children saw the black and white outlines as colours too.

When I talked with individual children about the picture, without mentioning colours, it was obvious in their replies that they saw many familiar items in colour. They compared them to the toys in the garden as I had done, even suggesting that the ball wasn't ours because we don't have one with stripes.

The activity gives you an insight into children's ability to think visually and, with a simple scene as in the park picture, it can provide plenty of opportunities for developing children's skills in the Early Years Foundation Stage.

Knowledge and understanding of the world is encouraged by talking about trees and flowers in their natural environment, what they need to grow and how we can care for them.

Communication, language and literacy will be enhanced by giving children time to think about ideas, express their thoughts, and initiate conversations related to the picture and their own experiences.

Problem-solving, reasoning and numeracy are developed by noticing and counting the apples or pears in the tree or by comparing (are there more pears than flowers or apples?), or by measuring the strings on the balloon and kite.

Physical development can be boosted by suggesting that each child use the toys outdoors like an obstacle course: climb up the slide three times then bounce, kick or throw the ball four times, run around the garden or playground to the count of five and travel around on a scooter or tricycle to the count of ten. Then rest and decide which one is most fun!

Creative development will be increased by focusing children's attention on tiny details, such as the flowers, the flames on the candles or the ribbons on the kite. Careful observation is extremely helpful in developing artistic skills.

Personal, social and emotional development can be promoted by showing the children how we need to use slides, balls and other toys with care and consideration of other children and adults. It also gives each child the opportunity to express their thoughts and experiences at the park or in the garden while having time to listen to and respect other children's opinions and ideas.

During the years I've worked in early years education, I have often found myself searching for a rhyme or song that 'gels' with the theme my group is exploring. Most times I find just what I've been looking for, other times there doesn't seem to be anything remotely connected to my topic, so I would resort to making up a rhyme or simple song of my own. I always used the tunes I knew and felt comfortable singing. I also found that if I was struggling to remember what I had just made up, the children would come to my rescue with their own versions of rhyming words. Sometimes they worked, more often than not, they didn't. But we all had fun in the process and learnt a lot about sounds.

If the words didn't make sense – it didn't matter. The point was to listen for rhyming words. Children love the activity – the sillier the rhyming words sound, the more the ideas flow. When a 'real' word is spoken, write it down and then choose from the best to make your song.

One way of encouraging this skill initially is to find objects around your setting that 'match' in sound, i.e. a cat, a hat, a mat. Add a few adjectives – toy cat, black cat, woolly hat, bright blue hat, woven mat or rolled-up mat. Then start rhyming.

'A big black cat with a woolly hat hides herself under the woven mat'. Or maybe it's not a cat but a 'furry kitten with a brown woollen mitten'. Perhaps that's how the three little kittens rhyme started life.

'A warm overcoat hides a plastic green boat'. 'The sun in the sky with a kite flying by', could begin or end a rhyme.

We devised the 'Colour rhymes activity page' with this idea in mind. The pictures give children visual clues for rhyming. They all rhyme with a specific colour as well as other words.

There are many rhymes that are simple and straightforward couplets to use when experimenting with making new rhymes. I think the original sources will be obvious as you read each rhyme.

Roses are red, the sky is blue,
Where, oh where, have I left my shoe?
Roses are pink and also red,
Can you see any growing under my bed?

Hickory Dickory Down,
The man has a coat of brown,
He went to town,
Wearing a frown,
Hickory Dickory Down.

Let's go fly a kite,
Up where the clouds are white,
Let's go fly a kite and send it soaring, etc.

Have a play with rhyming words, whether non-sensical or sensible, the children will go with it because it's fun!

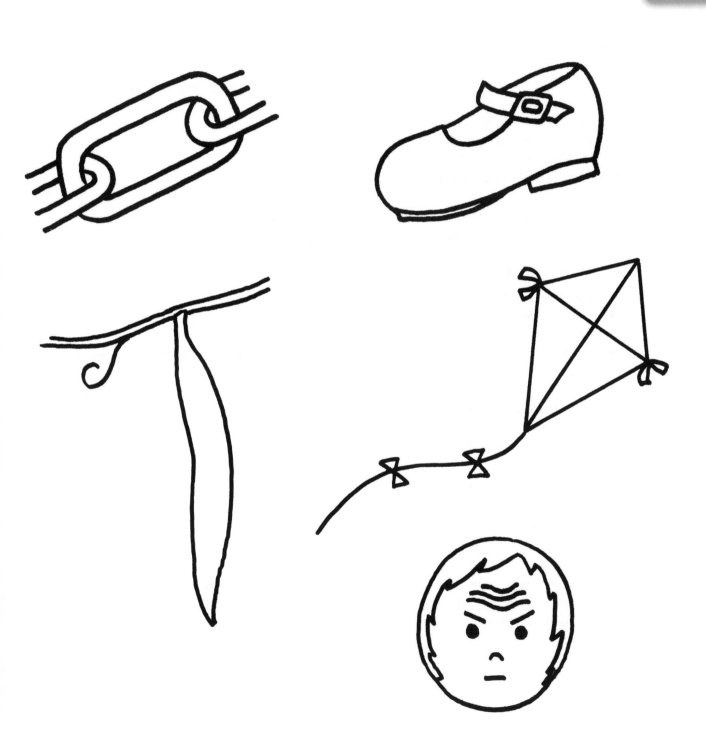

Games

The 'Games page' is designed to be a versatile piece of equipment.

Left as it is for a memory game or a guessing game. Coloured in – many other games can be played.

The memory game

Ingredients
A card photocopy of the page, scissors and a tray large enough to hold all the pictures required.

Method
1. Cut out the 'cards' and place face upwards on the tray.
2. Show the children the images for 30 seconds, asking them to remember as many of the pictures as they can.
3. Take away the tray.
4. Remove one image and replace the tray.
5. Which one is missing?
6. Replace that missing picture and start again.

Alternatively place the pictures on any flat surface and ask the children to cover or close their eyes before you remove a picture.

To simplify the activity:

- Use only two, three or four pictures.
- Choose images that are very different from each other.
- Choose pictures similar to each other.
- Name each picture as you place it down on the tray – this gives the children a verbal as well as a visual clue.
- Place the cards in straight rows or groups. The 'gap' of the missing card will be more obvious and therefore easier to remember.
- Give clues as to the object that has been taken – it bounces, it will blow away without string to hold, it shines in the sky, etc.

To increase the level of difficulty:

- Alter the position of some of the pictures when you replace the 'missing' card.
- Place the pictures randomly rather than in rows or groups. Remembering images that are 'dotted around' requires a higher level of concentration and is a more challenging activity when one is removed.
- Remove two pictures rather than one each time you remove the tray. Initially choose two images that are very different from each other. Then images that are linked in some way.
- Try these ideas out yourself, or with colleagues – they're not as easy as they seem.

Guessing game

This can be similar to 'I spy' only with cards that are placed, image upwards, on a flat surface. You, or the child, choose a picture (without letting the other person know which one it is), then give a clue to guess the object: e.g. it has petals, it grows on a tree, or it begins with the letter 'b'.

Giving a clue or describing an object is not always easy for us to do. Imagine how difficult it is for children. However, the clues will give you valuable insights into their level of development, reasoning and understanding.

Games page

Add colour to the pictures on the 'Games page' to give a further dimension to the activities that can be played.

Some of the images may suggest a certain colour, while others are less obvious. The idea is that many of the images can be lots of colours. If the game is played in summer, you and the children may think the leaf should be green, but in autumn you may decide on red, orange, brown or yellow. Caterpillars are often depicted as green. However, looking in books or on the Internet will show an array of coloured caterpillars.

Most of the images can be filled in with two or more colours so that the mixing, matching and comparing of the pictures becomes more varied. Duplicate the page, colour those images differently, and the activities they could be used for are increased yet again.

Snap

We all know how to play 'Snap' – matching pictures that are the same. How about 'Snap' where you match colours, not pictures?

This activity requires planning and forethought on your part as an early years' practitioner, but will provide opportunities for each child to develop their skills in observation, thinking and imagining, discussion and comparison, concentration and working together.

Only use one page of coloured pictures initially. Colour the images so that comparisons can be made between two pictures: e.g. the lollipop may be green with a brown stick; the caterpillar could be green and brown.

When first introducing an activity like this to a child, spread the cards out so that they can be seen easily. Chat about the colours to focus the child's attention and suggest that there are pairs that match. The butterfly coloured pink and purple matches the flower – they match – 'SNAP'. The yacht is red, yellow and blue, so is the house – they match – 'SNAP'. As the idea catches on, 'Snap' becomes a new game, and with more pages coloured and added, it can be played in a group situation too!

Association game

Dominoes with a difference.

Ingredients
Two photocopies on card of the 'Games page', crayons and scissors.

Method
1. Colour the pictures so that there are no duplicates.
2. Cut the 'dominoes' so that you have different pairs from each photocopy: e.g. caterpillar and star/caterpillar and leaf.
3. Play as dominoes. The connecting pair can be different pictures but associated in some way. In this way, there are very few 'wrong' associations.

In our group, one child put the umbrella next to the sunshine – why? Her mummy is always prepared – she uses her umbrella as a sunshade!

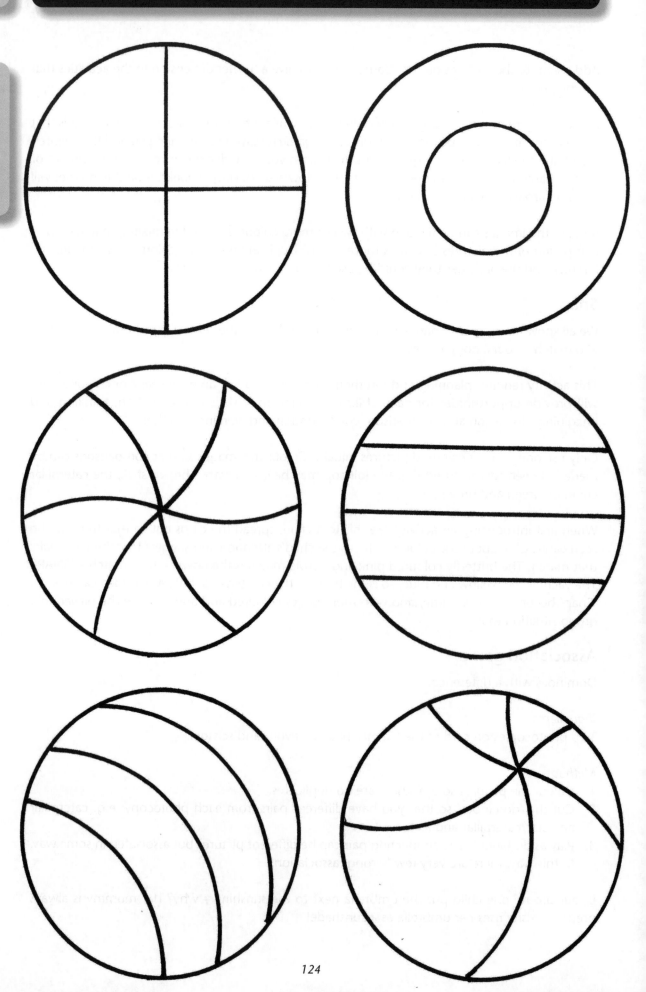

A favourite activity at some of the early years' settings where I have worked has been to make spinners. They can be used in place of a dice if shaped as a hexagon but also, and best of all, they can be colourful wheels which create delightful patterns as they spin.

The 'Spinning wheels page' shows six designs which can be photocopied onto card and cut out. Each section should be coloured differently using at least two colours so that when the wheels are spun, the colours blend together.

Make the spinning tops by piercing a hole through the centre of the wheel large enough for a spent matchstick to fit through. Experiment with the length of 'stick' required to get the best spin. Does the wheel spin better positioned halfway along the spindle? What happens if the wheel is nearer the top or bottom of the spindle?

Try using bamboo kebab skewers with a pointed end as the spindle. Does the spinner work better when there is a pointed end to turn on?

> **TIP**
> Children must be closely supervised when using any type of stick – even matchsticks. They are easily put in mouths, up noses, in ears etc., and kebab sticks, with pointed ends, can be potentially harmful. The finished spinning wheels should never be carried around because of the danger the sticks could cause to others. If a child makes a spinner to take home, always remove the spindle and hand it to the carer while explaining the need for supervision when using the spinners, before they leave your care.

Younger children, whose fine manipulative skills are still developing, may find their spinning wheel difficult to twist and spin using a matchstick. For them to be able to spin their wheel, we devised a simple spindle base.

Ingredients
A square of corrugated card (larger than the diameter of the wheel), a matchstick (or similar), a bead that will thread onto the stick, and glue.

Method
1. Push the end of the 'stick' into the centre of the card. This is the base. Glue the stick in place if necessary.
2. Thread a bead onto the stick, then place the wheel on top.
3. Hold the base with one hand and spin the wheel with the other hand.

> **TIP**
> If the wheel does not spin smoothly, increase slightly the size of the hole in the centre of the wheel.

For different effects:
• Decrease or enlarge the size of one or two of the stripes or segments.
• Increase or decrease the number of colours used.
• Repeat colours.
• Add dots or shapes of colour rather than fill the areas completely.

Colourful displays

When entering most early years' settings I am always amazed by the variety, imagination and inspiration displayed on walls, notice boards, tables and units. The displays are usually very colourful, eye-catching and show the children's work to great advantage with borders, double mounts, beautiful writing and appropriate labels together with 'hands-on' activities.

One colour display I have seen in many settings is of a colourful clown holding a bunch of balloons with the colour name on each balloon. Why not add the colour names to the clown's clothing as well, then the display can be used for matching colours and words too? Add coloured lengths of yarn to one word and give a child the opportunity of moving the string to matching the colour or the word – a display with more than one purpose.

Flowers are a popular display for a colour theme, on a table or wall. Why not try a flower garden outdoors? Paint plastic flowerpots in a variety of colours and fill with sand or soil. Cut acetate into flower shapes and paint each one a different colour. When the flower heads are dry, staple or glue them to a stick and 'plant' in the appropriate coloured pot. The flowers and pots can also be used for matching, sorting, comparing and one-to-one correspondence games and activities as well as being a very colourful display.

> **TIP**
>
> If the paint will not 'stick' to the plastic pots or acetate, try adding a little PVA glue or acrylic paint to the mixed paint.

Colour charts are displayed alongside alphabet friezes, number lines and pictorial time-lines for children to refer to. How often do they actually look at them, unless directed? Often they are out-of-reach, hidden behind a unit, incomplete because the 'sticky' on the back has come off or they have been there so long that the edges are torn and bent and no one notices them anymore. Shut your eyes and take time to 'look' at your setting – what can you remember? Does it catch your eye?

How is your information for parents, certificates, insurances, long and short term planning displayed? If we want notices to be noticed, why don't we put much thought or imagination into these displays? They can enhance your early years' setting and are often one of the first impressions people have of your premises.

During a colour theme over several weeks, we mounted our activity plans on corresponding coloured paper, written in appropriate colours. Notices and certificates required to be on permanent display were decorated with the 'colour of the week' crepe paper strips. It only took a few minutes to make a difference, and parents actually noticed their notices!

Section 2: Red

	KUW	CLL	PSRN	C	P	PSE
110 About red	•	•				•
111 Spotting ladybirds	•	•	•			
112 Spotting ladybirds page	•	•				
113 Seeing red, being red	•	•		•		•
114 Red-letter day		•	•			•
115 Dice template page					•	
116 Cherry tree game			•		•	•
117 Cherry tree game page					•	
118 Displaying red	•	•		•		

About red

Yellow, orange and red are known as the 'warm colours', with red itself perhaps the hottest!

Red grabs your attention and is one colour that is easy to see from a distance. This is one of the reasons why red is used to warn against danger. Flashing red lights denote danger or emergency; flashing red lights at level crossings or fire stations mean you must stop. Stop signs and traffic lights are red to get drivers' attention and alert them to dangers ahead and to stop. Look around for and chat with your group about other examples of where red denotes danger.

Many fruits and vegetables are red: tomatoes, peppers, radishes and an assortment of berries. Have a taste table to see which 'red' is preferred. Make a block graph featuring each child's observational drawing of their favourite red taste.

Emotions associated with red can lead to contradictions. A 'red-letter day', the 'red carpet treatment' and 'paint the town red' suggest important, special or significant occasions that need to be celebrated, whereas 'seeing red' implies being angry. A 'red herring' sets out to deceive or distract attention from the truth and a 'red flag' denotes danger and a warning.

You can be red with embarrassment, in the red and red-eyed – all evoke different meanings to the colour red.

It has been known for business people and other VIPs to wear red ties, as red can mean power and success.

Sports cars that are red evoke exuberance, speed and action. Look through magazines and make a colourful collage with the images of cars that the children spot. Are there more red than blue? Do silver cars feature more than red?

Red is also the colour of blood and identifies many organisations and charities that use red in their logos: The Red Cross, The British Heart Foundation and Leukaemia Research are a few examples.

Because red is such a noticeable colour, it is used in many well-known branded products. Put a notice (in red or on red paper) on the parents' notice board to ask for pictures, photographs or packaging featuring red in logos.

As many of the children in our early years' settings do not read, it is quite amazing how many of them recognise familiar words from adverts, TV and their local shops: Tesco®, T.K.Maxx™, Kellogg's®, Coca-Cola® and Woolworths® (now no longer on our high streets) were just a few they mentioned in one of our groups.

When I first glanced at the 'Spotting ladybirds page', I wondered where the matching pairs had gone. Christine and I had devised a similar idea several years ago with butterflies. We thought that the activities and games we played with those cards would work equally well with ladybirds.

We used them for the activities below as well as playing snap and pairs and happy families (with two photocopied pages). You will probably think of other games too!

The page is best photocopied onto card for durability and each 'card' cut out. The ladybirds should be coloured in so that their spots become more obvious.

> **TIP**
>
> Ladybirds can be colours other than red and black, so this activity page may be reintroduced when yellow, black, orange or cream are covered in your colour theme. Sometimes their spots are like eyes with a black pupil in the middle. Bearing in mind copyright issues, an Internet search will provide more pictures or photographs.

Let's count

Ladybirds (of which there at least 45 species in Britain) come in many guises but all have the distinctive spots on them. Whenever one is 'spotted' there is always a temptation to count its spots. With these ladybirds each child can do just that, matching and comparing as they count, perhaps even writing the appropriate numeral on the ladybird's back or head. By adding extra spots to a ladybird, children can begin to understand simple addition – and one more makes . . . ?

Comparing

Observe and discuss the differences in size of spots as well as the number on each ladybird's back to encourage children to notice that each ladybird has a matching pair.

Put one pair of ladybirds with one other ladybird card, mix them about and spot the different one – the odd one out.

Put one pair of ladybirds with up to five different ladybird cards, mix them about and find the pair again – find one the same.

These activities are important in developing visual discrimination skills to help in many areas of the Early Years Foundation stage.

What about beetles?

Discuss how ladybirds are part of the family of beetles and, as part of that family, are the most liked because of their colours. Gardeners especially like them because they eat greenfly on plants in the garden. They are also members of the insect family as they have six legs, wings and a segmented body. Their wings are under their hard shells which they lift to spread the wings and fly away. Their colourful red wing cases are a warning to birds that they do not taste particularly nice.

Spotting ladybirds page

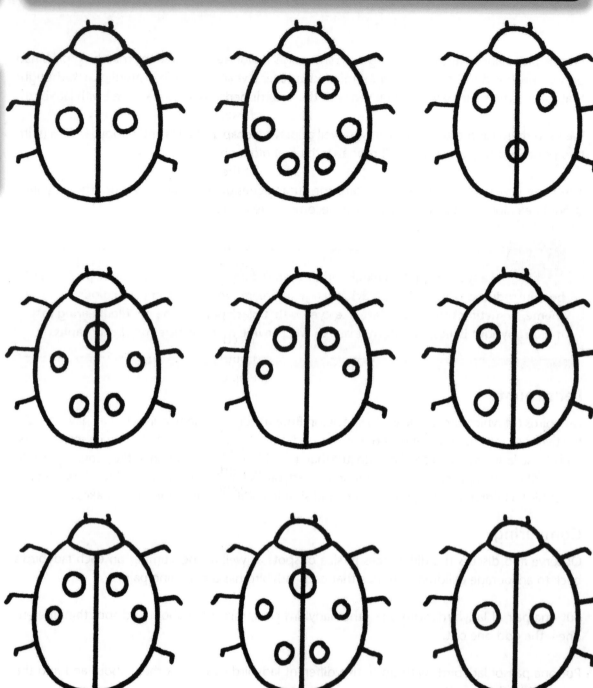

One of the most popular and imaginative play areas that we ever had was a red bus. We utilised lots of plastic red chairs placed behind each other in rows of two. There was also a chair at the front for the driver. Almost as soon as the 'bus' was finished, the seats filled up and, with a cap on her head, the driver said we were off to Blackpool to see the lights. Emily had just spent a weekend there and wanted to show us the beach with donkeys, like the postcards she'd brought in for us to look at. We paddled in the very cold sea and 'oohed' and 'aahed' at the lights in our imaginations. The journey back was extremely quick but the conversations on the coach home were full of holidays, favourite flavour of ice cream, names of donkeys, etc., and we'd only been gone for twenty minutes!

As this became a popular 'play corner' we added cardboard painted sides to the bus; a conductor often travelled with a handful of tickets to give to passengers, and of course no journey was complete without singing 'The Wheels on the Bus go Round and Round'.

'Red' is a great theme for play-corner activities. Another good idea is to make a fire engine (just as we constructed our bus). Children's play can be enhanced by singing 'Five Little Fire-fighters', or our version, five strong fire-fighters. Acting putting out fires, rescuing a cat from a tree or climbing ladders (a climbing frame or slide) all help develop children's abilities to solve problems, think logically, and use their imaginations as well as having a thoroughly good time.

The playhouse could just as easily become Grandmother's cottage in *Little Red Riding Hood*. No elaborate equipment is required at all, just a few children with an understanding of the story and a willing 'wolf'. Of course, you can always add a basket, cardboard ears on a headband, spectacles with large eyes drawn on, long plastic teeth (have hygienic wipes close at hand) and a square of red fabric for the cloak.

When a real postman's hat was given to our group, it sparked off so much interest in letter-writing that our play corner became a post office with used stamps (and gluesticks), paper, envelopes, writing pads, date stamps and ink pad, a till and money, telephones and tables and, believe it or not, a queue! We made a simple post-box, painted red with collection times on it, and brought indoors a red (and yellow) tricycle for the 'postie' to use delivering letters to the children.

Red-letter day

Communication between people has never been easier, quicker or simpler – with telephones, mobile phones, texts and e-mails. However, there is nothing quite like hearing the letterbox snap and the sound of a letter or card landing on the floor.

I love receiving mail and am often disappointed when the post is all for my husband. When we had our post office play corner with its post-box outside, the children loved posting letters with their friends' names on and then waiting excitedly for delivery time to see if there was a letter for them.

Our red-letter day game was devised so that a child could understand the process of writing and posting a letter.

Ingredients
Sheets of paper, pencils, envelopes and used stamps, one for each participant of the game, a photocopy (on card) of the 'Dice template page', scissors, glue and plenty of patience.

Method (to make the dice)
1. Cut out the box template, fold along the lines and glue the flaps to the sides of the box and leave to dry.
2. Cut out each picture and glue one onto each side of the dice. Once the glue has dried, the dice is ready for play.

One aim of the game is for each child to actually write a letter, by collecting the 'ingredients' needed to make it, and post it in a play corner post-box.

How to play
1. Each child takes it in turn to throw the dice.
2. If the dice shows a sheet of paper when thrown, the child collects a piece of paper to begin the letter.
3. The next item needs to be a pencil. The letter cannot be written without a pencil.
4. The picture of the letter is needed next and the child can start to write to a friend.
5. Then an envelope is required to put the letter inside.
6. When the address appears on the dice, the child's friend's name is written on the envelope they have collected.
7. All that is left to do is glue a stamp on the envelope once that picture is thrown on the dice.
8. Then post.

Once children understand the sequencing of letter writing, the order can change. For instance, if the initial throw is an envelope or pencil the child can collect either to begin their letter. Plenty of discussion may take place as to whether a stamp can be collected before the envelope that is needed to stick it to and, without a pencil, how can a letter or name be written on an envelope. Just the thing to start developing thinking skills!

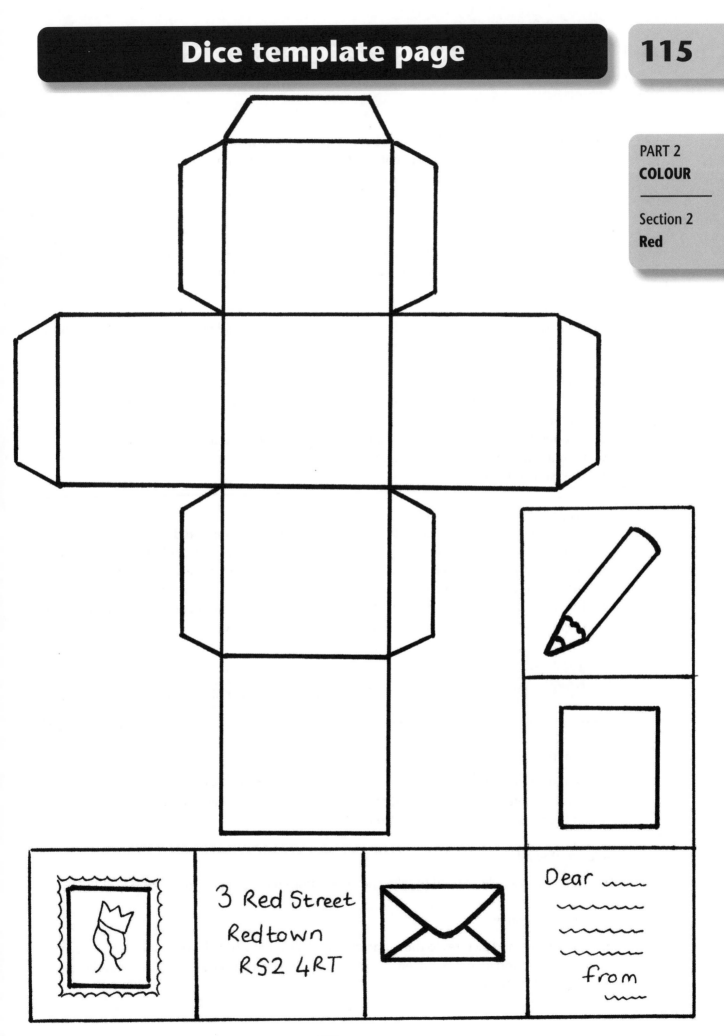

PART 2
COLOUR

Section 2
Red

3 Red Street
Redtown
RS2 4RT

Dear ~~~~

from

Cherry tree game

We were chatting with the children about red fruits and vegetables, discussing where and when they grew. Many children know that apples came from trees and strawberries grow on the ground, but what of other berries, fruits and cherries? We talked about how berries need protection to prevent the birds from eating them all before we pick them to eat.

One child told us how his dad had picked a cherry from the tree in the garden and there were two stuck together and one of the cherries had a bit missing. His dad had told him that a bird had already had a snack of his fruit, and the cherry tree game was born!

Ingredients
A photocopy on card of the 'Cherry tree game page' for each child playing, a dice or old wooden cube, crayons or felt pens, scissors and glue.

Method
1. Cut across the card to separate the tree from the counters. This becomes the board. The tree can be coloured if necessary.
2. Cut out the 'dice' squares and stick them onto the dice or cube.
3. Colour and cut out the cherry counters.
4. The game is ready to play.

How to play – the simplest version
1. Decide who throws the dice first – the eldest? Someone wearing 'red'?
2. Each child takes turns to throw the dice. '1' on the dice means the child can choose a cherry counter to put onto their tree. A bird means that the child misses a go (if they have no cherries on their tree) or a cherry counter is taken from the tree to be eaten by the bird.
3. The game is played until one tree is full of cherries or everyone is frustrated because the birds keep removing the cherries before anyone can fill their board.

> **TIP**
> You can always replace one of the birds with a '1' if the game is slow.

For a more challenging game:

- Change two (or three) of the '1's on the dice – add the numeral 2 (twice) and 3 instead. If those numerals show when the dice is thrown, only the counters with two or three cherries on them can be chosen to be put on the tree.

Add another rule:

- The birds are only allowed to take one cherry from the tree at a time – not one counter.

For a quicker game:

- Change the bird pictures to the numerals 2 and 3 so that when the dice is thrown, a counter is only ever added, not removed, from the tree. The child chooses a counter with the corresponding number of cherries on it.

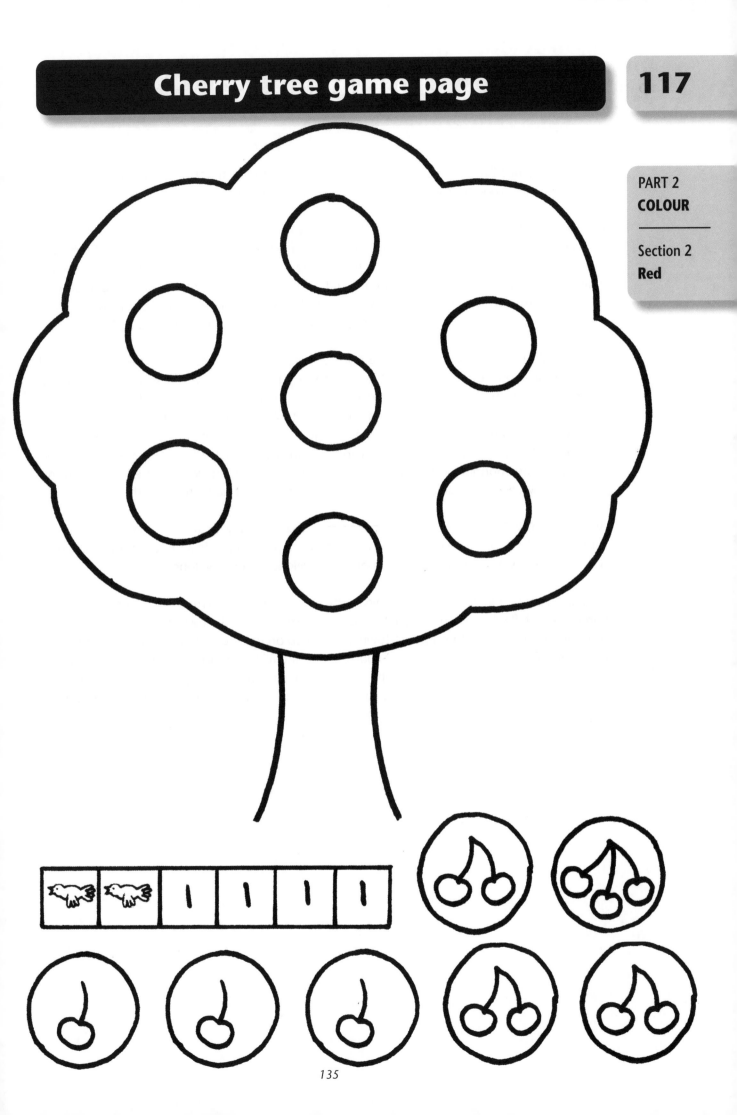

135

Displaying red

A red display need not be just 'red' things found at home or in your setting. Displays can be designed by incorporating songs or even characters from stories.

Collages are an extremely effective and striking way of depicting one colour. If you look around your craft area, paper store or bits and bobs box you will find an assortment of reds. Crepe and tissue papers are rarely the same shade, so add a few pieces of foil and cellophane from sweet wrappers and you will have several different red colours. Ferret out some scraps of fabric, strands of wool and thread and you already have the ingredients necessary to make a wonderful collage, either for a large display made with a group or for individual children to make a picture.

One red display we created involved a huge strawberry, decorated with hundreds of bits of paper, fabric and wool. It measured at least a metre in height and took most of one morning to complete. Some children just added two or three pieces of wool or paper while others stopped longer to fill in a larger area. It began on a circular table but quickly ended up on the floor so that the middle part could be reached by everyone. The children were very proud of the finished strawberry. The display also had drawings and paintings of a variety of animals. We had adapted the story of the enormous turnip for this activity. However, no one was required to pull up this gigantic strawberry because all the animals that came to see it had a feast on the soft flesh.

Another display featuring red was inspired by the 'Red-letter day' activity. We painted all the red Mr Men and Little Misses walking along a pavement to post a letter in a red pillarbox. The letters had either red writing with a red stamp on the envelope or the envelope was red.

We had a float in our local carnival one year. The theme was *Alice in Wonderland* and the children, parents and staff who took part were the playing cards painting the roses red. We sang the song throughout the journey through the town and carried on the theme back at nursery the following week. We had paper roses (red, of course) adorning all the shrubs in the nursery garden, we had them stuck on the fences and even in tubs on the playground. Crepe paper is wonderful for making rosettes and peonies as well as roses. They wouldn't win any prizes at Chelsea but make very effective flowers that are easy for children to make.

Section 3: Yellow

	KUW	CLL	PSRN	C	P	PSE
119 About yellow	•	•				
120 Colour associations		•	•	•		
121 Colour associations page		•				
122 Tying yellow ribbons	•			•	•	
123 Oak tree threading card page					•	
124 The sunny flower game	•	•			•	•
125 The sunny flower game page					•	
126 More sunny activities		•	•		•	
127 Yellow play	•	•		•	•	•

About yellow

Yellow is the colour of sunshine and suggests summer.

Yellow draws your attention and, like red, is used to signify potential danger. Because of its high visibility, yellow is often used for hazard signs and emergency vehicles. It forewarns us of construction work and vehicles too.

There are a few fruits and vegetables and many flowers that are yellow. Forsythia and crocuses end our winter, with daffodils heralding spring. Buttercups and daisies with the help of tall sunflowers mean that summer is here, and then autumn gives us worn-out leaves with shades of yellow.

There are many conflicting emotions associated with yellow. It can denote happiness, joy and cheeriness and can lift your mood, but is also the colour of cowardice, deceit and illness. Displaying a yellow ribbon shows hope and support, whereas the saying 'yellow-bellied' suggests a streak of cowardliness. If you describe someone as 'mellow yellow', they are usually relaxed and laid back.

Yellow is used to attract the eye and many adverts and logos feature yellow as a background to black: e.g. Yellow Pages telephone directory, Morrison's® supermarket and, of course, New York cabs. Petrol station logos can be very striking – BP initials were yellow set against a green background until 2001 when it introduced its green petalled flower with bright yellow petals around a white circle that we are all familiar with now. Shell petrol stations have had a very colourful logo since 1948; the shell is drawn in red with a startling yellow 'filling'.

When we talked about 'brands' with the children, all except three mentioned McDonald's – they all recognise the initial 'M' and its very bright yellow colour. We practised writing the letter 'm' in the air, then took a brush for a walk with yellow paint on it, making yellow arches and undulating patterns on A3 sheets of paper. Before the paint dried, we took a brush with red paint on it and repeated the pattern next to the yellow line; where the colours overlapped and blended slightly, orange was made.

We added blue paint to the mix and left the children to their own devices. Some wonderful colour blends and patterns were achieved with the children just taking their paintbrush for a walk. One child, using only red and yellow, did criss-crosses all over his paper. One diagonal was red, the other yellow and the blend of colour in the middle varied, depending on whether the first colour had dried slightly or not before the second colour was added. No two crosses were the same, and the final picture was stunning. Quite amazing what a four-year-old, a paintbrush, a large sheet of paper and two colours of paint can produce!

Colour associations

The 'Colour associations page' is for developing observational and drawing skills.

Most, if not all, the pictures on the page are associated with the colour yellow. Two or three of the images are simple outlines that can be observed and copied by the majority of children. Each child needs the ability to control a pencil or crayon and to look closely at the shape of the object before he will be able to draw a similar image with any accuracy.

Children begin to draw and write by scribbling, usually making light and feathery marks on paper. As holding pencils becomes more familiar and comfortable, the marks made are heavier and firmer, often in a circular pattern (scribbling) or backwards and forwards across the paper. Until children have learnt what they can do with a pencil or crayon and how to control it, there should be no expectations for them to begin an activity that involves observational drawing. A child needs to understand that he can lift his crayon and place it somewhere else to carry on making marks separate from each other before he can begin to draw 'pictures'.

Straight lines, dots and zigzags begin to emerge next to random scribbles, and circles often appear accidentally while the child is making random swirls. Vertical lines, straight lines and kisses (x) seem to flow at this stage in a child's development, alongside the circles. But copying a vertical cross (+) can be very difficult for a young child.

Once the child deliberately draws a circle with control, often eyes and a mouth, and maybe arms, are added to make a person. Add radiating straight lines to another circle and a simple sun is drawn.

Experiment with circles and straight lines to see what can be drawn and copied before expecting little ones to manage more complex observational drawing activities.

The images on the 'Colour associations page' can have other purposes.

- Very simply, photocopy the page and colour the pictures to fill odd minutes in the day.
- Enlarge some images for painting or collage activities.
- For counting – petals and points, leaves and dots.
- Make two photocopies and add 'extras' to one of the 'pairs' and spot the differences between them.
- Enlarge one or two of the images onto thicker card and make tracing cards or templates for the children to draw around.
- Make a number line of daffodils, all coloured different shades of yellow or cream.

The list is by no means exhaustive. There will be ideas throughout the book for you and your group to find other uses for these pictures. Keep a look-out!

Colour associations page

I'm old enough to remember the chart-topping hit for Tony Orlando and Dawn in 1973, called 'Tie A Yellow Ribbon Round the Ole Oak Tree', and knowing that yellow ribbons signify hope, support and remembrance, it gave me the idea for this next activity.

Threading card

Ingredients
A copy of the 'Oak tree threading card page' on thick card, yellow wool and a blunt-ended needle or yellow string or raffia, crayons or felt pens, scissors and a hole punch.

> **TIP** The threading card will last longer if you use mountboard card which can be cut with a craft knife. Or, if using thick card, cut out the tree and laminate it before you make the holes for threading.

Method
1. Cut out the tree shape and colour if necessary, not forgetting the yellow ribbon.
2. Punch holes around the outline, either randomly or evenly, as required.

The tree is ready for sewing.

1. Thread the needle with the yellow wool.
2. Tie the other end through one of the holes so that the thread will not pull through while sewing.
3. Sew with a running stitch or overlap the edges to make a yellow border.

Making a lace

Ingredients
Wool or string, sticky tape and scissors.

Method
1. Place a piece of sticky tape (up to 10cm long) on a table, sticky side up.
2. Take your yellow yarn and hold it very firmly between your thumbs and index fingers.
3. Still holding the thread tightly, place one end of it onto one end of the tape.
4. Roll this end of tape over the thread and stick it in place, then continue rolling the tape very firmly over itself until you have a stiff 'needle' for threading.
5. Cut the thread to the length required.
6. Then cut the sticky tape end to leave a neat 'needle'.

Your 'lace' is ready to use with the threading card.

Colouring threads

White cotton string, bought in any DIY, hardware or craft store, can be dyed for a threading activity. For a permanent colour: use a cold water dye with fixer – follow the instructions given on the packet. For a non-waterproof colour: dip the string in yellow food colouring or ink, leave for a few minutes and then dry, or colour the string with felt tip pens – messy but great fun. Fasten each end of the string to paper to prevent too much movement while colouring. The colour will 'bleed' if the string gets wet.

Oak tree threading card page

142

The sunny flower game

Our sunny flower game was originally designed as a quick and simple activity to help develop fine motor control of pencils and crayons but it soon developed to incorporate several areas of the Early Years Foundation Stage. As we played the game with the children, they asked so many questions that needed explanation that other ideas sprang to mind using the same simple picture . . . here's the game to start us off!

Ingredients
A photocopy of 'The sunny flower game page' for each child participating in the game, yellow and green wax or lead crayons or felt pens, an old dice, self-adhesive labels and, depending on the size of the labels, scissors.

Method
1. Place a self-adhesive label on each face of the dice, cutting to fit. Draw a circle on three sides and colour yellow – this denotes the sun. Draw a raindrop on two sides to represent the rain. The other side is left blank. The dice is ready for play.
2. Decide who will throw the dice first. Perhaps a child wearing something yellow to match the theme or someone with a flower on their shoes, etc.
3. If, when the dice is thrown, it shows a sun or raindrop, one petal can be coloured in yellow. If there is no picture shown, the child has to wait a turn.
4. When every petal on the flower head is coloured, then the stem and leaves can be crayoned in green and the game has finished for that child.

Colouring in pictures has caused some controversy over the years: often thought of as a pointless exercise, stunting creativity, free expression and drawing.

However, I defend colouring because a number of skills that ultimately help children learn to write are required when colouring in an outline. Children need to be able to manipulate a pencil or crayon with dexterity and accuracy. Colouring in helps to develop an awareness of the pressure needed to make marks and develop smooth flowing lines as a precursor to writing. Concentration, perseverance and control are required to enable the child to 'keep within the lines' as well as finish the task. And, besides all that, it can be fun and many children enjoy it, so what can be so wrong with colouring in as an activity?

As a child, my summer holidays would not have been complete without a colouring book and crayons. As an adult, I still find it a relaxing, calming and a real 'chill out' activity, and using multi-coloured leaded crayons makes for very creative colouring!

PART 2
COLOUR

Section 3
Yellow

Problem-solving, reasoning and numeracy form a huge area of any child's development. 'The sunny flower game page' gave me lots of ideas in which to promote one or two numeracy skills in particular.

Rotating number line

The ten petals on our flower lend themselves to a different type of number line – one that rotates. Photocopy the picture onto stiff yellow card (or white, if you want to colour or paint the petals). Cut out the flower head and number each petal in order from 1 to 10, in a clockwise fashion so that each numeral can be read from the bottom petal (i.e. the numeral is upside down at the top of the flower). Add patterns of dots to each petal to help with number recognition. Place a long split-pin through the centre of the flower, add a washer and attach the flower around a stick so that the flower head can rotate.

Number bonds

Cut out individual petals from the flower to create new flower heads, thus encouraging the idea of number bonds. A flower with six petals and a flower with four can make a ten petalled flower, etc.

Sequencing

Divide the petals and colour them two shades of yellow for sequencing patterns; e.g. one light yellow, two dark, one light, two dark.

If you or a child in your group does not like colouring in, then cut out the petal shapes from coloured card or paper.

> **TIP**
> To make many petals quickly, staple several sheets of yellow paper together, draw one petal on the top sheet and cut it out. Very time saving!

By planting flower seeds in pots and giving them light and water, children will begin to understand the need for rain and sun to promote growth, enhancing their knowledge and understanding of the world.

To encourage creative development make a yellow grocery shop, selling only yellow fruit, flowers and vegetables. Or what would it be like living in a yellow submarine? This Beatles song is very repetitive and one that children really seem to enjoy. It is brilliant for playing tambourines or triangles and singing along to, as well as marching, to enhance children's gross motor skills.

All of the activities mentioned could not take place without the need for communication, language and literacy skills which go hand-in-hand with encouraging personal, social and emotional development.

Yellow play

Make the most of your displays – even less obvious ones. Have your menu for the day or week written on yellow paper, or with a yellow felt pen on white card mounted on a sheet of yellow or with a yellow border. Newsletters or notices can be printed on yellow paper, reminding parents of the ongoing topic.

The equipment you have in your setting will determine the type of activities where colour can be included. Here are a few ideas to get you started!

- Have yellow cars, lorries and bricks in your small world play area.
- Colour the water in your water tray with food colouring or ink. Ask parents for any out-of-date orange squash as this colours water very well, and when diluted in large amounts, appears yellow. Have a duck race – borrow plastic ducks if necessary.
- Put yellow sand toys in the sand box or bury yellow treasure to be found. If you use buttons, counters or beads, make sure the activity is closely supervised and that you know how many pieces of treasure are buried, to prevent objects being put in ears, etc.
- Draw yellow chalk lines outside in your playground or garden for children to follow.
- Play throwing and catching games with yellow hoops, quoits, beanbags and balls.
- Hang strands of yellow wool from fences, bushes or equipment for children to find and collect. Suggest they hang them again for you and their friends to find.

I have mentioned earlier about marching, singing and playing instruments to the Beatles 'Yellow Submarine' song. One time the children and I talked about living in a submarine and the neighbours next door, like in the song. The discussion involved talking about being in a small space for a long time and how difficult it would be, when one little boy decided he wouldn't like it. 'It'd be worse than our tent on holiday, when it didn't rain at least we could go to the beach!'

We made a mock-up of a yellow submarine in our play corner with three large, painted cardboard boxes stuck together, no windows and only a hole at the top for the periscope, made with kitchen roll tubes and mirrors. The children could go in and out through one end (which the staff member could see clearly).

It wasn't the most popular play corner we've made over the years. But three boys loved being hidden away and spent a great deal of time using the periscope in the semi-dark.

Section 4: Blue

About blue

Blue is a cold colour: 'blue with cold' usually means freezing! However, almost everyone likes some shade of blue; it can be calming and cool, strong and steadfast or light and friendly. A deep royal blue conveys richness, navy blue can look almost black and is warmer than the lighter blues. A dash of blue will cool down a hot red or orange and the contrast of blue and yellow will grab attention.

Blue is also a natural colour, from the blue of the sky or sea; it symbolises peace, escape and dreams. Blue can invoke strong emotions and is often associated with calm feelings, although Blues music is often characterised by melancholy melodies and words and sayings like 'feeling blue' or 'getting the blues'.

Blue can convey importance and confidence without being sombre or sinister, hence the blue power suit of the corporate world and the uniforms of police officers.

Red, white and blue is a patriotic colour trio for flags of many countries. Children love flags, to watch them flutter in the wind, to hold and wave and to place on top of a sandcastle. After explaining to some of the children in our group about flag days, we decided to have one of our own to celebrate Friday. We spent a lovely afternoon making flags on paper with red, white and blue on them. We used paint in the main but also self-adhesive stickers because, after the children had seen a photograph of the American and New Zealand flags, they wanted to add stars as well as stripes to their flags. We cut out five pointed stars from gummed paper for the children to glue onto their flags. As it wasn't raining on the Friday, we decided to staple the flags on our outside fence before the children and parents arrived. Their flag day began before they came through the door. We played national anthems of many countries throughout the day and, during chat time, the children decided that our nursery's anthem should be, 'If you're happy and you know it', as this had been a favourite song for a while!

The flags certainly drew a lot of attention from passers-by; two or three neighbours asked what was going on, loved the idea of just celebrating an ordinary day and wished they were four again so that they could join in. The flags were so eye-catching in the three colours that we looked through magazines and catalogues to show the children how colours can draw our attention.

This is a simple activity, fun to do, easy to organise and with plenty of scope to develop further. Give it a whirl!

Calm waters

The idea for 'The calm before the storm activity page' came about through talking with the children about the colour of the sea. Is it really blue? What about a river or stream or babbling brook? If you scoop up some water from the sea into a bucket, what colour is it? Why does it appear to be blue from a distance but the sand and shells can be seen through 'clear' water when you paddle at the beach?

Listening to the children's answers can give an insight into their general level of development and will help you decide on the type of follow-up questions to ask them and depth of information they will understand.

The simplest explanation is that the sea reflects the sky. However, it is not as simple as that. There is no single cause for the colours of the sea. They depend on the brightness of the sky, the concentration of particles suspended in the water and the position of the observer. The day it is overcast, the sea is generally more grey than blue and, similarly, when the sky is brilliant blue, the sea is also. The colour of sea water is largely produced by the absorption, refraction and reflection of light.

Either way, the next time you go for a dip in the sea, look closely. There's more to the colour of the water than meets the eye!

We used several sayings such as 'the calm before the storm', 'as quiet as an ocean front', 'the roaring sea' and 'as calm as a mill pond' to illustrate the idea of 'moods' of water. And we realised that as we spoke, we automatically moved our fingers, hands and arms to 'express' the meanings of each saying and what we were talking about. After listening to some extracts from Mendelssohn's 'Fingal's Cave' and Johann Strauss's 'Blue Danube', we 'became' the sea; lying flat on the floor, making little swishing sounds like the waves lapping the sand, right through to rolling and rocking all over the floor as a storm. We sang as many 'sea' songs as we could remember, rowing boats and travelling the oceans.

Once on dry land, we devised 'The calm before the storm activity page' to help develop children's fine motor skills. 'Trace' with fingers first for smooth movements, then use tracing paper and pencils or acetate sheets and felt pens, attached to a photocopy of the page by paper clips. The idea is to follow the lines from left to right (as though on the surface of the sea), beginning very calmly on the mill pond, to swishing over the waves and then being on the raging sea at the end.

The calm before the storm activity page

When you look around your early years' setting, how many things do you see that are blue? Often display tables are full of the things that are found around the room or brought in from home. With a little forethought and imagination, your display table can become much more 'hands on' and inviting to children.

Musical blue table

Ingredients
Cardboard tubes, a selection of 'fillings' – rice, spaghetti, pasta, small pebbles or gravel, beads, buttons, blue paint or papers, glue, sticky tape and scissors.

> **TIP** I always asked parents or staff to look in their cupboards for out-of-date pasta, etc., or we would buy split packets from supermarkets if using food for craft activities. Ethically I couldn't justify using fresh products when 'old' food items could be used for this purpose.

Method
1. Seal one end of each tube with a circle of card, cut to fit, and sticky tape in place.
2. Paint or cover each tube in blue paper – the more shades available, the more striking the display.
3. Put equal amounts of one 'filling' into two tubes. Do not overfill or the sound the shaker makes will be dull. Seal the ends. The pair of tubes does not have to be the same colour. It actually adds to the difficulty of the activity if they are dissimilar.
4. Fill two more tubes with another sound and seal the ends. Repeat with as many tubes as you have painted or coloured.
5. Mix them all up and put them into pairs that match, either by shades of blue or by shaking each tube and finding its matching sound.

It's not as easy as it sounds!

Book display

A student made a lovely display with all the blue *Mr Men* and *Little Miss* books (by Roger Hargreaves). She and the children created finger puppets and cardboard cut-out figures which stood up by supporting stands. The children enjoyed making up stories and playing with these Mr and Miss figures throughout each day and were sad when 'blue' became 'green'.

Colour book

A favourite, often permanent, display was our book. At the beginning of many topics, we made a book from sugar paper. It was placed on a table for children to add their thoughts, pictures or photographs. The front cover always stated quite clearly the theme, and parents, visitors and students were invited to add their ideas too. Whenever our theme was a colour, we usually had to add more pages because the children often did a picture for the book, rather than take it home.

In and out the dusty bluebells

When I lived in Scotland, we always sang 'In and out of the Scottish bluebells' when we played this game in the playground. I later found out that in other parts of the country, the song is called dusty or dusky bluebells. However, the way it is played is exactly the same wherever you live.

All that is required for the game are willing participants, space and a little bit of singing.

* Everybody joins hands and makes a large circle facing inwards.
* Someone is chosen as 'the leader' and stands in the middle.
* The children in the circle raise their arms to make arches.
* The leader sings the first verse while skipping in and out of the circle, under the raised arms.

> In and out the dusty bluebells
> In and out the dusty bluebells
> In and out the dusty bluebells
> I am the leader.

When the verse ends, the leader stands behind the person nearest to them and pats very gently on their shoulder.

The person whose shoulders are being tapped sings the second verse.

> Pit-a-pat, pit-a-pat on my shoulder
> Pit-a-pat, pit-a-pat on my shoulder
> Pit-a-pat, pit-a-pat on my shoulder
> I am the leader.

This child becomes the leader with the 'first leader' following behind, holding the new leader's waist. The whole process is repeated. Each time, the leader sings the first verse with the other 'leaders' following behind.

Play carries on until there are not enough children left to make a circle.

An alternative version
It takes a great deal of confidence to sing on your own, especially if you are concentrating on moving in and out of people and under arches.

Most early years' settings play group or ring games and so we used the same idea with this activity. Once a leader was chosen, everyone joined in with the singing of the verses, adding the leader's name to the last line, e.g. 'Mary is the leader'. When the leader tapped the shoulders of another child, we included their name in the last line of the second verse. Then the leaders would swap places with each other in the circle.

Obviously, if a child feels confident to sing by herself, then we all remained quiet and let her weave in and out, singing away, only prompting if necessary.

We all know that balloons come in lots of different colours and shapes. They can be great fun to play with indoors and are usually a 'hit' with most children (and adults). Whenever beginning an activity involving balloons, always check that the children are comfortable around them, maybe finding a different but similar activity for the one or two who are not.

One nursery I worked at had visited the theatre with a group of children, and during the interval a couple of people dressed in very colourful costumes were walking up and down the aisles, making dogs and hats out of balloons for the children to take home. Most of the modelled balloons survived until the children arrived back at nursery where they were admired by everyone. The following weekend I managed to buy some modelling balloons. They seemed stronger and definitely more flexible than ordinary 'birthday' balloons. The balloons were long and very narrow and came with instructions on twisting them together. There were one or two pictures of models that could be made, including a flower and butterfly. After a little practice at blowing the balloons up, I made a hat with two of them. They twisted together quite easily and I felt that a number of children at nursery would enjoy having a go.

So that is exactly what happened. There were some weird and wonderful models. Some children just enjoyed the experience of twisting one balloon around itself, others made simple hats and, later on in the day, our 'after-schoolers' made animals, wigwams, spiders and a lobster!

Blue Balloons puzzle

The 'Balloons puzzle page' can be used for any colour, today it's blue.

Ingredients
A photocopy of the 'Balloons puzzle page' on card, five different blue felt pens or wax and lead crayons and a craft knife.

Method
1. Colour each balloon a different shade of blue.
2. Very carefully cut out each balloon with the craft knife (do not cut out the triangular 'ends' and string) so that you are left with a 'frame' and five balloon pieces.
3. The puzzle is ready for use – just fit the balloons in the gaps.

This may seem an extremely easy puzzle to complete. However, careful observation of shape, size and orientation is required to fit all the pieces in the right places. Once the balloons are muddled up, the three of similar shape are difficult to distinguish from each other. Try it yourself to see.

Alternatively you can just cut the image into two or more pieces. Curved line edged pieces are easier to fit together than straight lines, and obviously the more pieces there are, the more difficult it is to put the picture back together again.

Colouring all five balloons in the same colour blue will also add to the difficulty of the puzzle.

Balloons puzzle page

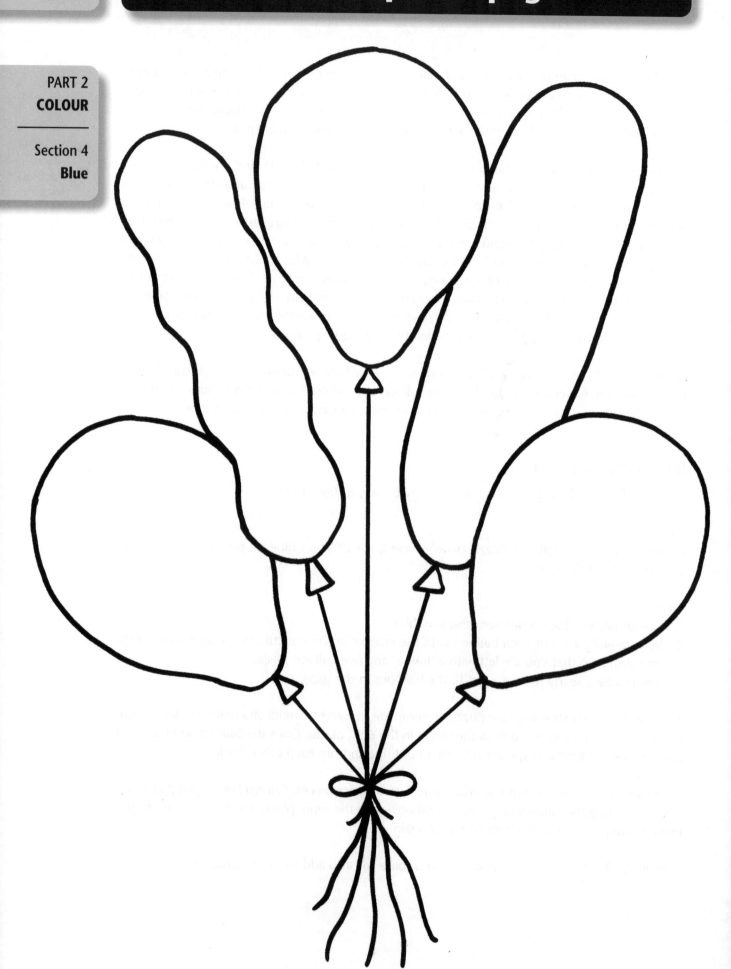

Let's look out for blues

When deciding on a blue colour activity several years ago, I was struck by the amount of equipment around the room that was not of one single colour. Until I asked a child to find something blue, I must admit I hadn't really taken much notice of the colours of the toys around me. This particular day, my little box of bits and bobs (see 'Tips and shortcuts') had been left in another room and I thought the task of finding one blue object would be relatively easy. It wasn't.

Amy looked around the shelves and came back with a box of wooden beads containing an assortment of colours. If we had been in another room she might have found a blue maracas in the music trolley or a pair of blue mittens in the dressing-up box, perhaps a blue bucket or spade in the sand tray. However, I was presented with the box of beads, and what followed developed into the blue game, although it could be used for any colour.

Amy decided that she wanted to see how many blue beads were in the box. Then she remembered the tub of plastic buttons, 'I think there's more blue ones in there.' Off she went to find out. There were more blue buttons than blue beads. Then the Duplo® was investigated and I thought of a game, either for one child or a small group to play.

The 'Finding blues game page' has seven pictures of commonly used items found around an early years' setting. However, if your group has no buttons or pegs, then discard that image and choose a picture from another activity page that is more suitable.

Photocopy the page onto card and cut out each square. Place the 'dots' in one pile and the pictures in a separate pile, both face downwards. The child picks a card from each pile, finds the object shown in the picture and then produces the correct number to correspond to the dots on their second card.

You may need more 'dot' cards to play the game with a larger group of children, why not write numerals onto cut squares of card or photocopy another sheet and add extra dots to make larger numbers.

Carry on the activity outdoors using beanbags, quoits, balls or hoops. Try draping strips of blue crepe paper, strands of wool or feathers around the walls and fences or shrubs and flowers. Ask children to find a specific number, a bit like an egg hunt, and don't forget the other colours!

Finding blues game page

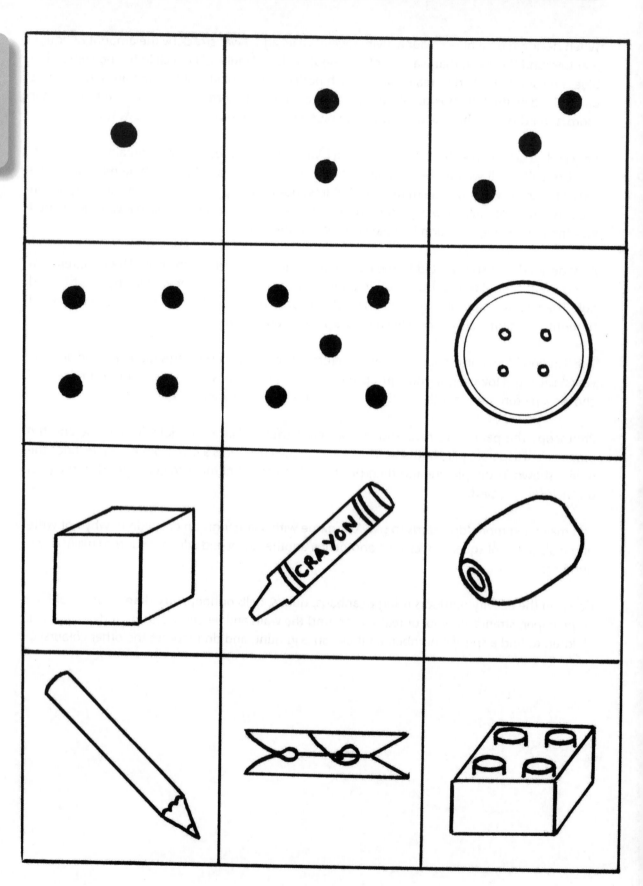

Section 5: Green

	KUW	CLL	PSRN	C	P	PSE
137 About green	•	•				
138 Traffic lights	•	•			•	
139 Rainforest café	•	•		•		•
140 Caterpillar game			•			•
141 Caterpillar game page					•	
142 How green is your shopping?	•	•				•
143 When I went shopping page		•			•	
144 Five green frogs		•	•	•	•	•
145 Five frogs, a log and some bugs page		•			•	

About green

Green can have both a warming and cooling effect. Green very often represents life. It is abundant in nature and signifies growth and has strong connotations as a colour and symbol of conservation, ecology and concern for the environment. Both Greenpeace and Oxfam have green logos, as does the Green Party.

Green is a restful colour as it has some of the calming attributes of blue which can create a feeling of ambience. The 'green room' is where actors and guests relax before or after a performance at the theatre or on TV.

Since the eighteenth century, gambling, billiard, snooker and table tennis tables have been green as it was associated with victory and defeat, instability and ephemeral qualities.

Green is often the colour of camouflage.

To be a 'green-eyed monster' or 'green with envy' suggests jealousy, and to be 'green-fingered' means you are good with plants and gardening. To be 'green behind the ears' implies that you are inexperienced, untrained or a novice, whereas 'greener pastures' are associated with something new or better.

Green is the national colour of Ireland, and St Patrick's Day wouldn't be the same without shamrocks and green-costumed leprechauns.

I love the word 'evergreen' – it's a perfect description. When discussing 'green' words with a group of children, they came out with some inventive ones too! One young man was quite indignant that his mum's lime-green car wasn't green like a lime and, 'She won't believe me!' When we arrived back at our pre-school setting after visiting our local greengrocer, we had to explain to several concerned children that the grocer sells lots of fruit and vegetables, not all of them green. How confusing our language can be! Words don't always seem to mean what they say or describe.

Another trip we took when 'doing' our colour theme was to a DIY store to look at all the different types of paint and their names. Each child was able to select several colour chart strips which we took back to nursery. After reading some of the colour names, we decided to make our own colour charts with names for a display.

Each child started with a light base colour to which they could add some green paint. There were three different shades – a light green, a bright green and a darker green. Eventually, the colours were mixed, painted onto sheets of paper and left to dry. No two colours were the same and when displayed looked very effective on the wall. Most children chose a name for their colour, some were amusing. We had lime and caterpillar green, bottle and broad-bean green, Dan's peppery green and sprouting spinach green.

If you are 'given the green light', it usually means you have permission to proceed. With traffic lights on green you can drive on if the way is clear, although pedestrians who are already crossing the road still have right of way.

When playing the game of traffic lights in the playground or indoors, the rules are slightly different – green means GO whatever! Amber means slow down ready to stop, and red means stop immediately but, as with real traffic lights, it depends on the speed you are doing as you slow down as to whether you can stop in time.

The main difference between real traffic lights and the game is the fact that traffic lights are in a particular sequence with a set number of seconds between them, giving advance notice. In the game, whoever is saying the three colours, can take several seconds, or longer, before calling out the next colour. The sequence of colours in the game is always the same, however, so children will soon become aware that after green is amber, then red, then green again. They understand that green means go, amber means slow down to stop, and red means stop and you need to hear 'green' before starting again.

There are several alternatives to this game: red means sit down, green means jump around, amber means touch the ground.

- Red for stop, green for hop, amber (or orange) for drop (to the ground).
- Red means talk (stop and chat with a friend), green means walk and amber means chalk (on paving slabs or sugar paper)

> **TIP**
> Using words that rhyme in the game will help children to remember the actions to be taken when each colour is called out.

Many ideas are interchangeable, even as the game is played. Often each child likes the chance to be the traffic light caller. So we decided that they had up to ten 'calls' before someone else changed places with them. When a 'new' traffic light was introduced, they could choose what each colour would mean in their game.

Have a selection of small apparatus available around the garden or room for the next few ideas.

- Amber – pick up a beanbag, green – walk around with it on your head or between your knees, red – put the beanbag back in the place you found it.
- Green – run, amber – turn around and go the other way, red – stop.
- Red – jump into a hoop (sharing hoops is good), green – jump out, amber – run about.

All these activities promote and develop skills in concentration, listening and memory, alongside having fun.

Rainforest café

Play corners were one of the most popular activities in all the early years' settings where I've worked. They take the children to another place, another experience and give them opportunities to be another person.

I have often thought about doing other jobs, swapping with someone else for a month, just to feel what it is like to be in another person's shoes. Obviously there are some professions and places of work where it would be impossible to change places with someone, but in play corners children can dabble with ideas and begin to get some sense of different types of work.

I'm not suggesting for one minute that your play corners should look like the real thing. However, I am suggesting that you, as an early years' practitioner, should play alongside the children, especially when a new idea is being introduced, so that you can explain what this new environment is all about.

Imagine yourself in an unfamiliar working environment. The other people in the room seem busy walking around with bits of paper, answering the phone, and there doesn't seem to be anyone to ask for advice. What would you do? Make a few notes? Pick up the phone and chat with your mum? Or sit down and look fed up? I saw this happen when a student opened an office in our nursery. She spent over an hour setting it up. She supplied everything, it looked very efficient and professional, a lovely inviting play corner. However, when the children came to work, she left them to it. The children enjoyed themselves, drawing pictures and chatting to each other on the phones, but what did they understand about working in an office? The children needed guidance, and you need to observe them playing to know when to join in, when to offer advice or help and when to leave them to it.

Before we made our rainforest café we spent time talking about rainforests: the wildlife, the protection of habitats, deforestation and climate change. When we were making the café, several children became very involved with it, helping to decide what sort of pictures should be displayed.

The walls were covered with pictures of monkeys and apes, toucans and macaws, snakes, butterflies and frogs, many painted by the children themselves. The pictures were hidden behind large sugar paper green leaves and vines and creepers (made from paper strips) that hung from the walls. A large piece of camouflage material was used as a canopy roof, making the café quite dark and atmospheric. The menus showed pictures of food and drink available, and with a table, chairs and our play kitchen, our rainforest café was up and running.

This is a quick and simple game that you can use to fill a few spare minutes or when playing group games in your setting. The idea is that the caterpillar needs the green leaves to eat and grow.

Ingredients
A photocopy of the 'Caterpillar game page' and the 'Dice template page' on card, green crayons (optional), scissors, glue and counters.

> **TIP**   If you photocopy the 'Caterpillar game page' onto green card, no colouring will be necessary.

To make a simple board game

Method
1. Cut out the dice template, leaves and caterpillar (cut straight across the page underneath the caterpillar to make the playing board).
2. Colour the leaves green if required and glue onto five sides of the dice template.
3. Fold the template along the lines and make into a dice.
4. The game is ready for playing.

How to play
1. Each child is given a counter (button or piece of paper) as their playing piece and places them on the caterpillar's head. Always ensure that the children know which colour counter is their own.
2. Decide who goes first, perhaps the child who first throws an ash tree leaf on the dice.
3. When the dice is thrown and shows a leaf, the child can move his counter to the first segment of the caterpillar's body. If a blank side shows on the dice, the child's counter cannot move. Play continues in this way, moving a counter if a leaf shows on the dice and missing a go if the dice side is blank.
4. The caterpillar is fully fed when the first counter reaches the last segment and the game ends.

To make a game for each child to play individually (or in a group)

Method
1. Cut out the dice template and add a leaf to five sides. Fold along the lines and make into a dice.
2. Cut out the caterpillar's segments and head – nine pieces in total. If children are cutting out the caterpillar, the feelers on the top of its head can be snipped off for ease of cutting (they are only of cosmetic value to the board game).

How to play
1. The child starts with a caterpillar's head. Every time a leaf appears when the dice is thrown, the child can add a segment to his caterpillar to make it grow.
2. The more leaves, the bigger the caterpillar!

Additional ideas
• Add numerals to each segment, so as the caterpillar grows, a number line is made.
• If the blank side shows, take a segment away instead of missing a go.

Caterpillar game page

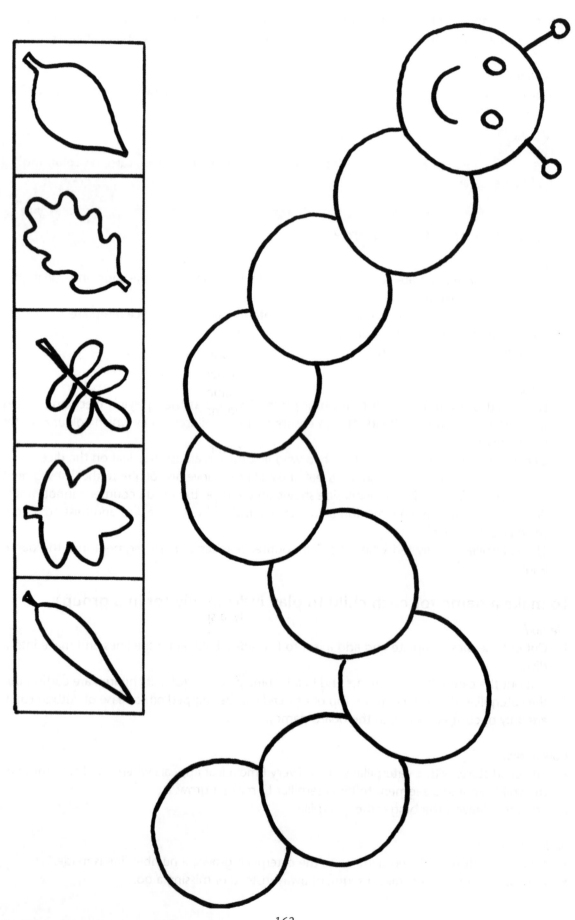

How green is your shopping?

I can remember when I was in the Brownies playing a game called 'When I went shopping'. We all sat in a circle and Brown Owl usually started us off by saying, 'When I went shopping I bought a dozen eggs.' The Brownie on her left would then add her bought item to Brown Owl's eggs, e.g. a dozen eggs and cheese. The next person would continue by adding another item to the growing list. The game continued until a Brownie could not remember all the items in the right order.

I have often played the game since with our after-schoolers who had an amazing capacity for remembering the items. We used a theme for the shopping list, only allowing items that had been bought in a specific type of shop: sport, greengrocer or pet shop, to name just three.

Our 'When I went shopping page' grew out of this memory game. The activity page is designed to help and encourage younger children in the development of language, listening, concentration and memory skills. Very often children will repeat what has been said by their near neighbour but may have difficulty remembering the order of items previously. When children are thinking about 'adding on' another item at the same time, the skills required are multiplied. Giving a visual clue will create a link between their auditory memory and their communication skills.

Photocopy and cut out the separate images on the page and let each child choose one picture, giving them a visual clue to their item and others. The activity is played in the same way but if a child has difficulty remembering an item as they go along, the picture can be shown as a prompt to memory. The images we have used are, in the main, thought of as green.

Obviously there are some pictures that could be any colour and this is one way of developing the activity.

The pictures can be coloured to give extra visual clues and information for the children to use when they add to the shopping list; for example:

'When I went shopping I bought . . .'

- With an added colour – a blue pencil, a red balloon, an orange jelly, etc.
- By adding an adjective to the image – a wobbly jelly, a spiky plant, an open book.
- Using two words to describe the picture – a soft yellow pear, a crunchy chewy toffee.

There are other ideas within the book where these images can be used for other purposes. Mix and match!

When I went shopping page

Five green frogs

A storyboard is an extremely valuable piece of equipment in any early years' setting and can be used to great advantage in the following activity.

The rhymes

Use the rhyme 'Five little speckled frogs sat on a speckled log, eating some most delicious flies'. There are several versions of this song, so the frogs on the 'Five frogs, a log and some bugs page' are not speckled. Speckles or other embellishments can be added to the photocopy by yourself or the children to match the version of the song you normally sing.

Similarly, some of the flies are bugs too!

Ingredients
A photocopy of the 'Five frogs, a log and some bugs page' (preferably on card), crayons, scissors and whichever 'sticking' attachment you use on your storyboard.

Method
1. Colour and cut out the frogs, bugs and log.
2. Attach Velcro®, white-tac, sandpaper or felt to the back of each picture.
3. The song is ready to be enacted. Place the five frogs on top of the log, with the bugs above them.
4. As the song is sung, each frog, in turn, jumps into the pool until there are no frogs sitting on the log.

The same frogs can be used for singing and enacting another frog rhyme: 'Five green frogs sitting on a well'.

> Five green frogs sitting on a well,
> When one looked up and down he fell.
> Frogs can jump high, frogs also jump low,
> Four green frogs sitting on a well.

Displays

We once made a huge ten-foot-long display of a log with five green frogs sitting on it. They all had concertina paper arms and legs attached to a very simple frog-shaped body with big bulging eyes. The flies were made from fluffy black fabric glued to kitchen roll tubes (cut into three) with tissue paper wings and hung from the ceiling in front of the frogs.

It wasn't the most artistic display but it was the children's own work. It was bright and colourful and a bit quirky but caught everyone's attention as they came into the building and usually made them smile.

Puppets and plays

A ring of cardboard can be stuck to the back of the frogs cut out from the photocopy (onto card) to make simple finger puppets that each child can use to enact the rhyme during circle or story time.

Make masks from paper plates that have been painted. Cut out holes for each child to see through and add additional circles to the top edge of the plate as the frog's eyes. Attach a band to the plate around a child's head and encourage them to enact the rhyme for their friends.

Five frogs, a log and some bugs page

Section 6: Orange

	KUW	CLL	PSRN	C	P	PSE
146 About orange	•	•				
147 Bumblebees	•		•	•	•	
148 Bumblebee template page					•	
149 Orange segments			•	•		•
150 Matching segment slices page	•	•				
151 Oranges are not the only fruit	•					•
152 Oranges and lemons	•	•			•	
153 Fruit bowl fun		•	•	•	•	

About orange

Orange is a combination of red and yellow, so it shares some common attributes with these colours. Orange has less intensity or aggression than red because it is calmed by the cheerfulness of yellow.

As a warm colour, orange is a stimulant and conjures up images of Vitamin C and good health.

Orange is found in nature – autumn leaves, the setting sun, and the skin and meat of citrus fruits.

Because of its high visual impact, orange is an important colour in matters of safety and is used in the manufacture of life jackets, rafts and buoys, as well as the boats of the RNLI, the Royal National Lifeboat Institution. Experiments done by NASA have discovered that orange is the most visible colour to use on a spacesuit and is the last colour to disappear in darkness.

During an orange week at nursery, all our snacks were orange. We had sliced, diced and shredded carrots and pepper rings. Luckily it was during the early summer when apricots, peaches and nectarines were plentiful and cheap. Of course we didn't forget the family of oranges. As we were unable to buy a pumpkin, our cook made a tomato and carrot soup which turned out to be delicious and quite orangey in colour.

When we looked through magazines and catalogues, the children spotted Sainsbury's® almost immediately and then chatted about the shelf labels, carrier bags and uniforms (without any prompting) – several of the children's parents worked at our local supermarket and had obviously visited it many times. Several staff members shopped there and had never really noticed the colour of the notices and labels – I do now! The mobile phone company Orange® has a strong visual impact in the high street and its advertising on TV and in magazines is difficult to miss.

One colour activity I clearly remember involved using sweet wrappers. We had made some very simple kaleidoscopes with kitchen roll tubes, perspex, small pieces of cellophane sweet wrappers and sequins. The children were holding them up to the light when one child shouted, 'I've made orange!' She was so excited that she rushed from the room to go and show her friends. She came back soon afterwards almost in tears. The shapes had moved in between the plastic sheets as she went out of the room, and by the time she met up with her friends, her orange had disappeared. I explained how the coloured cellophanes had overlapped and made new colours. We found some larger pieces of cellophane and experimented to make new colours, especially orange.

The mixing colours activity continued for a few days, overflowing into mixing paints and other crafty materials. Some absolutely stunning pictures were made by the children using red and yellow paints with sponges and rolled-up kitchen paper or tissues. The effect was even more startling when the background was black or deep blue.

We experimented with wax and lead crayons, felt pens and watercolour crayons on different paper to create a variety of colour blends, and one of our favourites was using chalks on the paving slabs in our garden and on sugar paper. Occasionally the results were 'muddy'. This often happened when too many colours were swirled together on the paper. Occasionally it occurred when too much of a deep or dark colour was added to a lighter one.

We also used tissue paper and watered-down PVA glue. The tissue paper was placed on sheets of perspex and covered with a layer of glue. More tissue paper was added and another layer of glue. Once dry, the paper was transferred to the windows so that the full effect of the overlapping of colours could be seen.

When the tissue paper sheets were put onto the windows, the children 'saw' pictures in the different colours produced, and one young man said one of the colours looked like a wasp. One step further and we were making stained-glass bumblebees.

Ingredients
Orange, yellow and red tissue paper, PVA glue, water, large brushes, sheets of perspex or plastic sheeting (available from DIY stores: paint protector), scissors, photocopy of 'Bumblebee template page', black sugar paper or painted paper, stapler and staples.

Method
1. Staple the photocopied template onto several sheets of black paper so that as you cut one bee, you cut several.

> **TIP**
> The stripes of the bee can be cut with a craft knife, remember to always use a cutting board underneath to protect the surface of tables, etc. and replace the safety cap after use.

2. Spread the tissue paper onto the sheet of perspex or plastic and cover with watered-down PVA glue. Use a wide brush to spread the glue thinly and quickly. Larger brushes also prevent the tissue paper from creasing too much.
3. Place another layer of tissue paper on the top and brush over with more glue. Leave to dry overnight.
4. Peel the dried tissue paper from the perspex or plastic.
5. Stick strips of the coloured tissue onto a template. Glue a second template to the other side, if required. Cut tissue to shape for a neat-looking bee.
6. Display them on the windows of your setting.

Bumblebee template page

A number of children disliked oranges for a snack because of the pith that surrounds each segment; it can be quite chewy. Some children would try and peel off each tiny strand before eating it. So we avoided peeling oranges in this way by cutting each one in half around its 'equator' and then into slices. Offering circles and semi-circles of fruit was much more inviting to our youngsters, causing much less hassle too.

During an orange themed week we had a choice of citrus fruits for snacks. Satsumas, clementines, tangerines and oranges were all sliced ready when we noticed that they had different numbers of segments in the slices. One little mandarin orange had nine segments while one much larger orange had only seven. The children were fascinated by the idea that the oranges were not symmetrical. Some segments were much wider than others, even in the same piece of fruit.

Using orange paper, we drew around three circular objects of different circumferences, made a mark in the centre of each and then cut from the outer edge to the mark, making several segments. Then we put the circles back together again. The children liked the activity so much that they asked for more orange slices for them to cut. Eventually there were twelve different sized circles and an assortment of segments. It was extremely difficult to put the pieces back together, mainly due to the fact that the centre mark was sometimes missed and the sides of the segments did not match. Nevertheless, two children persevered until all the pieces fitted together and there were twelve slices of orange again. We drew matching symbols on the reverse of four of the more tricky oranges so that children could check they had the correct pieces if they wanted to re-do the puzzles.

The idea was adapted to produce the 'Matching segment slices page'. There are many ways the images can be used. A few are mentioned below, but try out your own ideas too!

- Photocopy the page onto orange card (to save colouring) if a child wants to make the orange slice puzzles as previously described. There will be two matching sets.
- Use the page for developing observational skills by finding matching slices.
- Add dots to each segment of one of the pairs and write the corresponding numeral on the other matching slice. Cut out each segment and place the numeral with its matching number of dots.
- Photocopy the page onto card, colour the segments on each slice and make spinners to see the colours blend or separate (see 'Spinning colours').

While working with children I have often been amazed at how TV affects their thinking and choice of activities. Many of the programmes are harmless and innocent, using different ways to grab the children's interest and attention, with puppets in *Sooty*, *Dora the Explorer* in cartoon format, and adults dressed up as the *Tweenies*. Other programmes are less obvious and children often cannot differentiate between the two. They sing and jump around with Josie Jump on *Balamory*, so why not copy other characters too.

I was in a pre-school recently when they banned children playing *Ben 10* because there had been several injuries when one or two children had thought they could emulate the actions on the TV screen. It reminded me of the 1980s, with *Teenage Mutant Ninja Turtles* and more recently in the early 1990s when *Power Rangers* hit our screens.

The advertisements interspersed with programmes can influence children too. They remember the jingles and one-liners and 'Oranges are not the only fruit' idea came from an incident that happened in 1991 during snack time when a child slapped his friend's face. The child responsible for the slap thought it was hilarious and couldn't understand why his friend was upset and hurt. When asked why he slapped his friend, he replied, 'You know when you've been tangoed' and carried on giggling. This advert had appeared, very briefly, to promote Tango®. While a chap was standing outside a shop with a can of Tango in his hand, a man painted orange runs around him and slaps his face immediately after he tasted the orange drink. The saying the child used sprang from the supposed feeling you get when you drink Tango (and being slapped in the face).

His friend was drinking apple juice, not orange! He replied that his dad had told him that oranges are not the only fruit that give you a slapped-face feeling. We thought we'd put that theory to the test by having a tasting session. We squeezed satsumas and clementines – no slapped-face feeling. We drank orange and apple juice – no slapped-face feeling. We tried peaches and nectarines liquidized – no slapped-face feeling. But when we drank some grapefruit juice, we sucked in our cheeks – but didn't slap any faces.

Dad couldn't explain what he had meant later when told about the incident with his son, but they both realised that the seemingly harmless advert was not something to be practised on other people.

Your taste session need not start like ours did; however, it can be useful in flexing our taste buds and descriptive powers!

Oranges and lemons

This nursery rhyme has been sung by children since before the eighteenth century when the lyrics were different and not as sinister as today's version.

The place names in the song correspond to various churches in and around central London, and the tune that accompanies the words suggests the ringing of the specific church bells.

In one of the earlier versions, 'Oranges and lemons say the bells of St Clement's' is not the first line of the song, but it does mention Whitechapel and St Margaret's. Another example of the rhyme mentions twelve London church bells, before the lyrics using six of those churches became a popular children's singing game.

As with the rhyme, there are several versions of the oranges and lemons singing game.

Game one

Two children face each other, clasp their partner's hands and raise their arms to make an arch. The players file through, in pairs. The challenge comes during the final lines:

> Here comes a candle to light you to bed.
> Here comes a chopper to chop off your head.
> (Chip chop, chip chop, the last man's dead.)

On the last word, the children forming the arch drop their arms to catch the pair of children who are passing through. These two children then make another arch next to the first one. The song is sung again and two more children are caught and make a further arch. In this way, the series of arches becomes a tunnel through which each pair of children have to run to escape being 'trapped'.

Alternatively:

- The children forming arches may bring their hands down for each word of the last line, while the children passing through the arches run as fast as they can to avoid being caught on the final word.
- The first pair of children to be caught change places with the original arch. Play carries on with the children making the arch changing every time until everyone has had a go.

Game two

Two children form an arch as in the previous game. One side of the arch is the Oranges, the other side, the Lemons. The other children skip around, passing under the arch as they sing the song. During the last line, the children forming the arch pretend to chip and chop as the children pass through. On the last word, the 'arch' drops their arms to catch a passing child. The child chooses whether to become an Orange or a Lemon, standing behind whichever side he has chosen. Repeat the game until everyone has been captured and is an Orange or a Lemon. Then the two teams have a tug-of-war.

The picture below can be used to boost several areas of development.

- As a tracing card to increase a child's fine motor skills, co-ordination and concentration.
- As a puzzle to encourage visual awareness and dexterity and promote problem-solving skills.
- As a counting and/or numbering activity.
- As inspiration for the following activity.

Paint ball pictures

We made some orange fruit bowl paintings long before tennis and cricket players started to sell their 'hits' as pictures. We were playing with sponge balls indoors when one happened to land in a paint tray set up for printing. A child lifted it out and, not realising how heavy it had become, dropped it on the floor. The result was an orange circular blob. It gave me an idea. We placed a sheet of paper on the floor and dropped the paint-filled sponge ball several times, making a group of oranges. When the painting was dry, we cut out the 'fruit' and painted a bowl for the oranges to sit in.

I never thought it would catch on with tennis players or cricketers, and they sell them! Examples can be found on a Google images Internet search.

Section 7: Brown

	KUW	CLL	PSRN	C	P	PSE
154 About brown	•	•				•
155 Autumnal weaving	•	•		•	•	
156 The chocolate cakes		•	•	•	•	•
157 Find two the same activity page	•					
158 The baker's shop	•	•	•	•	•	
159 Bark rubbings	•	•		•	•	
160 Shades of brown page		•				

Our reaction to colours is often instantaneous and can have a profound impact on the choices we make every day. There have been many investigations into the effects of colour on our behaviour and emotions.

Brown often conveys a feeling of warmth and is found extensively in nature, both in living things and inanimate materials. It represents wholesomeness, earthiness and dependability.

Although found in natural surroundings all year round, it is often considered an autumn and winter colour. I was made very aware of the autumnal colours surrounding brown when working in a special school many years ago.

I was talking about the different shades of leaves we had gathered from the trees outside when a three year old boy pulled on my arm for attention. He continued to pull on my jumper, pointing from my mouth to the leaves in front of us. This young man had been born with Treacher Collins syndrome, had no ears and could only sense vibrations. He was learning to communicate using the Paget Gorman Sign System which gives signers the opportunity to use grammatically correct English. I had learnt the basic colour name signs, i.e. yellow, orange, red, brown, which I had used while chatting with the group. He signed 'more words' to me as he realised that I was saying more than I was signing. He excitedly pointed to my mouth, to my signing dictionary and then the leaves. He fetched the dictionary and we learnt the signs for copper, bronze, auburn, chestnut, etc. and then wrote a note for his family about his new vocabulary.

Up until this point, I hadn't really thought about how many shades of brown there are. How bright, rich and warm they can be as well as very dark, almost black.

We use tan or beige as light-coloured backgrounds for mounting our displays, pictures or paintings, making them appear brighter or sharper, and dark brown adds a warmer tone than using black. So during a 'brown' week, I thought I'd put background browns to a test. We made a display for the children to decide which colour was most effective, using paper of various shades of brown laid on a display table with coloured objects on top of each sheet.

The children moved the items onto the background they thought made the object look best. Each child then put a self-adhesive dot matching the object's colour on the appropriate sheet of paper. At the end of the week we made a block chart of the results. Not very scientific I know, but enjoyed and appreciated by the children when they knew that their thoughts and feelings had been taken into account!

Autumnal weaving

The brown background activity led us on to using just strips of brown papers to make woven pictures.

Ingredients
Coloured paper strips, glue or double-sided tape, scissors, and a sheet of paper for the base.

Method
1. Place a strip of double-sided tape or glue along the top of the base sheet.
2. Stick one end of a paper strip to the glue or tape, starting at one edge so that the strip lies on top of the base sheet.
3. Continue sticking strips along the top until you reach the opposite edge – this is called the warp.

> **TIP**
> Ensure that each strip is separate from its neighbour, with a slight gap in between each strip. Weaving is difficult to do if the strips overlap.

4. Once the warp is complete, choose a strip of paper to weave over and under each of the vertical strips – this is the weft. To make the weaving neat, move the weft up the vertical strips (the warp) as near to the glued ends as possible.
5. Take another strip and weave under and over – the opposite of the previous strip.
6. Continue until the base sheet of paper or the warp strips are covered.
7. Finish the weaving by gluing strips along each edge of the woven papers as a border, trim away any excess paper.

To create different effects:

*   Add texture with assorted papers – handmade, metallic, sugar or painted or use strips of cellophane.
*   Tear the strips of paper, rather than cut, to give a softer edging.
*   Use a variety of widths for the strips, including shredded or quilling paper.
*   Leave gaps between the strips so that the base colour can be seen underneath.
*   Try cutting up cards or gift wrapping paper for a variety of colour.
*   Add shades of yellow, red and orange for a really autumnal finish.

We collected leaves and twigs on our trips to the park or out in the garden and added them to our finished weavings. Once the leaves were dry, some of the children wove the leaves through the warps and the wefts, others used glue. The brown display caught parents and visitors by surprise because the effects of the weavings were quite stunning to see.

'Five currant buns in a baker's shop' is often a favourite rhyme and action song in early years' settings. Children enjoy acting out the buying and selling of the buns. We always added extra verses, and our version mentioning chocolate on the top became more favoured by the children than a topping of cherries or sugar.

We made a subtle change of bun to cake and had even more verses to sing. The cakes were so appetising that we couldn't just take them from the shop in a paper bag – they had to be eaten straight away.

> Five brown cakes in a baker's shop
> Crunchy and munchy is the chocolate on the top.
> Along came . . . (add child's name) with a penny one day,
> Bought a tasty cake and ate it straight away!

After making some of these cakes with salt dough, they did look almost good enough to eat, so we decided to make some real cakes. We had a lot of mess, a bit of fun, but ended up with some very tasty cakes. Each child chose a cake to decorate and their name was written on the base of the paper case their cake was in, so there would be no confusion when taking them home or eating later. The children were able to choose up to three toppings from a selection: white icing, chocolate icing, coloured strands (similar to hundreds and thousands), chocolate strands, chocolate buttons, sugared jellies, etc.

When each child had finished adding bits to their cake, they were put on a table to 'set' and covered with muslin to prevent flies and fingers from touching.

Several children spent a great deal of time looking and comparing each other's iced cakes and making comments. 'I've got seven choc-chips on mine, you've got four.' 'Who put two buttons on that one?' and 'That one's boring – hasn't got coloured bits on it, just icing, nothing else.'

Listening to some of the statements the children made about the finished cakes gave Christine and I the spark of an idea. But when we heard, 'Hey, Charlie, look over 'ere. There ain't two the same, you know!' our idea was firmly formed and the 'Find two the same activity page' will always remind me of Joe.

The title of the activity is self-explanatory; however, as with many of the activity pages, adapt the images for your own requirements. A couple of suggestions:

- Colour, cut out and use with a storyboard and the rhyme above.
- Remove the cake case stripes from one of the 'same' cakes, making them all different. The child fills in the missing bits to make them all the same.

Find two the same activity page

The baker's shop

The previous activity spurred us on to making a baker's shop play corner. As with most ideas, we chatted with the children about what should be sold in our shop. And after several visits to our local bakery, as many of the children had only experienced the bread and cakes counters and shelves in the supermarkets, we decided what needed to be made. We ended up with loads of props because the children had so many ideas and were very enthusiastic. I think they hoped their play corner would smell as delicious as the bakery!

Because we baked our play-dough, many of the biscuits, buns and cakes lasted for months and were used in our café corners, tea shop and play picnics. All were made by the children – with a little help and a few suggestions.

The easiest, quickest and most effective props were our gingerbread biscuits. We used our gingerbread people cutters as templates for drawing around and then cut the shapes from light brown card. The children added brown and black dots and squares as eyes, buttons, etc.

Buns were made with a salt dough mixture, currants were added to some and glacé cherries to others before baking or leaving to air-dry. Alternatively, once a plain play-dough bun was dry or cooked, the children painted currants onto it. Some spread glue on the top, with a sprinkling of white glitter to represent a sugary topped bun. A chocolate button or flake can be added to the top of a cake by cutting out a small circle (the button) or a rectangle of brown paper rolled into a tube and secured to represent the flake.

We made chocolate and cream Swiss rolls out of some thin sponge sheets (from packaging). The sponge was cut into several strips, painted deep chocolate brown on the edges and one side and left to dry. With the 'chocolate' side face down, place a plain strip on top, roll the two together, trim the 'cream' and glue the roll securely for a chocolate roll.

> **TIP** Adding acrylic paint to powder paint will give a more lasting colour, without flaking.

Chocolate cakes were made by adding brown powder paint to the salt dough, put into paper cases and baked slowly in the oven. When they cooled down, the children painted icing of different colours on the top.

Salt dough was used to make the bread. One bread roll became a favourite to make by the children. They twisted two 'sausages' of dough and pinched the ends together. The dough does brown slightly when cooked; however, some children added brown paint for crusts!

Brown is a lovely colour to include in this theme but it is very often left out. It has so many shades that are found widely in nature.

Your setting may have painted doors and skirting boards, but I'm sure you or the children will be able to spot a few chips where the wood shows through. Even the grain will be different shades of brown. Collect some colour charts from a local DIY store to show the children how many browns are named after types of wood, e.g. mahogany, oak, hazel and beechnut. Have a go at mixing your own brown paints and give them appropriate names.

Outside in your garden or playground there may be wooden fences or even trees. If you have a flower bed or potted plants, collect some soil from each and notice the differences in the types of earth. Both are brown, but are they the same? Look closely at stones, pebbles and gravel to see numerous 'browns'.

Autumn is obviously an excellent time to collect browning leaves for displays, but look around in spring and summer too, as leaves drop throughout the year. Remember to look out for nut shells that the squirrels have left behind, as well as pine cones and conkers.

Look at sand through a magnifying glass to see the variation in shades of brown in the tiny grains.

I remember one autumn when a walk to the park had been planned to do some bark rubbings. Parents had been invited to help, we had our crayons, chalks and paper ready when the heavens opened and the rain started. It rained all morning, the parents went home but we still did our rubbings. Anything with a texture had paper put over it and was rubbed over. Ashleigh's shoes had tracks on them, they worked a treat. So did the blown vinyl wallpaper in the corridors!

Check out your brown wax and lead crayons. There are so many shades on the market that can enhance your theme. Dark and deep burnt sienna through orangey chestnut, russet and tan to lighter hues like fawn and beige. Don't forget the metallic crayons of copper and bronze to add a bit of shine to any rubbings.

The pictures on the 'Shades of brown page' are for a colouring-in activity. Although they could all be coloured with the same brown crayon, the pictures would have no depth. As with the ideas above, children need the opportunity to notice 'browns' in real objects to use coloured crayons effectively. Provide photographs and pictures from books and magazines or, if possible, the real thing to help with their observational techniques.

Section 8: Pink and purple

	KUW	CLL	PSRN	C	P	PSE
161 About pink	•	•	•	•	•	
162 About purple	•	•				
163 Two-way windmills		•		•	•	
164 Two-way windmill template page					•	
165 Food for thought	•	•	•	•	•	•
166 Matching patterns			•	•	•	
167 Matching patterns butterflies		•				
168 Rhythmical ribbons	•			•	•	

About pink

Colour is considered to be one of the most useful and powerful design tools that we have. People respond to different colours and shades of colour in a variety of ways. This was very evident when we decided to have a pink week. Many of the boys in our group were adamant that they would not use pink crayons or paint, paper or collage materials. Some would not even participate in activities involving anything pink because 'Yuck, that's for girls.'

Although many people think of pink as a feminine, soft and delicate colour, a favourite with girls, I was quite surprised by the boys' reactions. However, as we talked about the colour pink, many of the boys realised they did like pink sweets, e.g. bubblegum, marshmallows, candy floss and strawberry chews were all mentioned with grins. Most agreed that the flavour of pink was yummy, not yucky.

We went on to explain that pinks are shades of red, a colour most people like. Later that morning, we experimented to see how 'pink' a red had to be before they disliked the colour.

Ingredients
White and red paint, plastic containers, small brushes or spatulas, pipettes or syringes, aprons.

Method
1. Give each child a brush or spatula and a shallow plastic container with a teaspoonful of white paint in it.

> **TIP**
> The lids from tubes of Pringles® are ideal shallow containers for mixing the paints on and are easily cleaned to be used again. Ask parents to start saving them for you.

2. Pour red paint into the pipettes or syringes for the children to add one or two drops to their white paint.
3. Mix the paints together to make a new shade of red. The less red that is added, the paler the pink will be.

Some children were amazed at how few drops of red paint they needed for the colour to change to pink. We tried the same experiment by adding drops of liquid and powdered ink as well as food colouring into the white paint to see what would happen.

> **TIP**
> Always supervise the use of pipettes and syringes – they can be used like water pistols, and red inks and food colouring stain almost anything very easily. Always ensure children wear protective clothing when appropriate.

Children also noticed how some of the red paint stayed in the bristles of their brush, not always mixing with the white, so that when they used the paint later, there was often a lovely swirled streak of red/pink in their picture. Much admired by boys and girls alike.

About purple

The boys didn't share the same reticence with purple as they did with pink. They seemed to think it was a strong colour and were happy to join in with all the activities during our week of purple.

Purple is often associated with royalty, nobility, dignity and wealth, largely due to the fact that dyeing cloth purple was an expensive process and the garments were usually worn by high priests, emperors and leaders who could afford the fabric. Perhaps children can sense the richness of the colour?

A number of purple words refer to fruits or flowers. Lavender, lilac and violets are delicate and often considered quite precious, and aubergine, beetroot and pomegranate are three fruits and vegetables that signify deep, strong, purple colours.

When we were looking for purple pictures for a montage in adverts, magazines and catalogues, the children only came across Cadbury's Dairy Milk chocolate with its trademark gold writing. Pink logos and names were thin on the ground too but there were plenty of flowers and clothing pictures we could use.

Our purple and pink montages were added to our pink and purple paged book which was filled with extremely tasty looking collages of strawberry ice creams, candy floss and butterflies (see later ideas).

We made some lovely stained-glass windows in the shape of butterflies (using the same method as the orange bumblebee activity). We used pink and purple tissue paper but were very surprised when the colour in the purple quickly faded with the sunlight through the windows. The purple faded more quickly than the orange or yellow tissue paper, and when I spoke to a friend about it, wondering if she had experienced anything similar with particular colours, she couldn't give me any answers. What she did tell me was almost the reverse of what had happened with our tissue paper butterflies. She had heard that glass made without lead in the nineteenth century would turn light lavender if placed in a sunny window and that old glass placed in sand in the sun would turn purple which was irreversible.

Two-way windmills

I remember as a young child at the seaside building a sandcastle with my dad and elder brother and wanting something to stick in the top of it. We went to the beach shop to buy a pack of flags. However, when we reached the shop they had no flags left. My dad bought us a windmill instead. It was plastic and spun rapidly in the breeze off the sea.

When we got back to the castle, the windmill was far too large to fit on the sandcastle so my dad crafted a speedboat out of the sand with double seats at the front and back, enough for all four of us children to speed away in. The windmill took pride of place on the bow and we were so proud of our boat!

The windmill was only one colour and I told my mum that I thought how lovely and bright it would be if the windmill had been two colours.

The following day was very wet and we had to stay indoors. It was our holiday, which was in a static caravan by the sea, and four children under ten in a confined space for a few hours is no fun for anyone. After playing several board games and building with Lego®, I got out my crayons and colouring book, when my dad suggested that we made a windmill each. He unfastened the plastic windmill and used it as a template for us to draw around.

We all coloured the outlines differently, cut the corners and gently folded them towards the middle. My mum produced four pins from her needlework box and dad pinned our windmills to small pieces of driftwood left under the caravan. Of course, there was no breeze indoors so we had to blow or spin them with our fingers to move the windmills round.

This image has stayed with me and although nowadays you can buy windmills of two colours, making them is as popular today as it was when we were stuck inside our caravan.

Ingredients
A photocopy of the 'Two-way windmill template page' for each child, pink and purple crayons, scissors, glue, drawing pin or nail and piece of wood.

Method
1. Colour both sides of the square; use patterns to add to the effect.
2. Cut out the square and along the lines from each corner towards the middle.
3. Fold each marked corner into the middle and secure in place with a little glue.
4. Practitioners should place a pin or nail through the centre of the windmill, secure in a piece of wood and ensure the pointed end is safe.

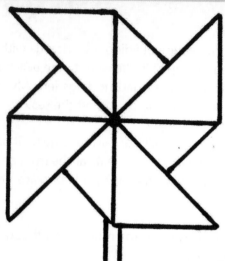

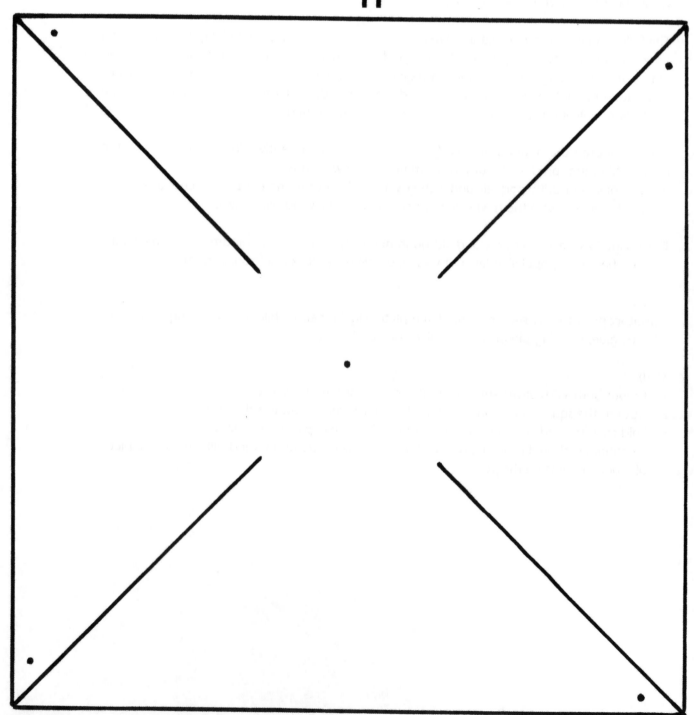

The boys gradually came round to thinking that pink was just another colour – not just for girls! And by adding purple into the mix helped to diminish any pink prejudices.

On one occasion the children voted to have a cookery week, where every day they'd be cooking or making something pink, purple or a mixture of the two. We sent out a letter to parents telling them of our plans and asking if they could loan any small cookery aprons: we knew the activity would be popular and only had four aprons of our own.

There are so many berries that are red through to black that become pink and purple when squashed, boiled or mixed together that we were spoilt for choice as to what we should make. Parents who grew their own fruit and vegetables kindly added to our basket of goodies and we were set.

We started off the week making jellies. I can remember the experience of making jelly with my mum. As we pulled the jelly cubes apart, we always ate one cube each, 'To strengthen our fingernails', she said! At nursery, we made jelly from cubes and powder, adding fruit to some dishes and leaving others plain. They were then placed in the fridge to set. Although a very easy activity to do, always ensure children are well supervised when using hot water.

On Tuesday we made trifles using a pink sponge made by our cook the previous day. Raspberries and blueberries were put on top of the diced sponge, then strawberry jelly and pink blancmange on top. We ate one trifle with our lunch . . . which was not pink or purple! And the others were eaten at snack time.

On Wednesday we cooked rhubarb crumble. While some children helped to make the rhubarb filling, others made the crumble mixture. Enthusiasm got the better of these children and they added pink food colouring to make the first pink crumble mixture I have ever seen. We put the cooked rhubarb into individual cake trays and spooned the mixture on top, enough for everyone to taste for snack time, or to take home to eat later for lunch or tea.

Thursday was pickling day, cooking beetroot to slice and bottle it with vinegar. Not such a popular activity but fascinating to watch how beetroot stains everything it touches – especially my white cookery apron!

On Friday we realised that we still had lots of fruit and vegetables left. Our cook made magnificent moussaka with the aubergines and a plum pudding for dessert, while we tasted blueberries, blackberries, raspberries, grapes, plums and strawberries at snack time.

Matching patterns

The following activities are based on the idea of symmetry in butterflies' wings. An Internet search will produce hundreds of images of butterflies for children to refer to, along with illustrations, pictures and photographs in books and on posters.

Butterfly prints

Ingredients
Painting or sugar paper, pink, purple and white paints, brushes, aprons.

Method
1. Fold the sheet of paper in half, then open it back out.
2. Paint or splash the pink and purple paints onto one half of the paper, adding drops of white paint as required.
3. Refold the paper and rub all over gently to spread the paint so that the paint blots are reproduced on the other side of the paper.
4. Open out the sheet.
5. Add more paint if required, following the steps above.
6. Once the paint has dried, fold the paper in half again and cut out wings to resemble one side of a butterfly. When the sheet is reopened, the wings of the butterfly will match.

Matching patterns

The butterflies on the 'Matching patterns butterflies' page are all the same shape and size but their wings are different from each other. The right and left hand wings of each butterfly need to match, so the activity involves careful observation and fine motor skills in order to complete each butterfly.

We used lines for simplicity of copying and circles because that is usually the first shape children begin to draw with ease.

The images can also be used to make the diagonally opposite butterflies exactly the same as each other. However, this does require a greater degree of observational experience than completing symmetrically opposed lines and shapes. Try it yourself and see.

Finger puppets

The finished butterflies were coloured in pinks and purples, although several children asked for browns, beiges and black to colour the butterflies' abdomens. They were quite happy to colour the wings brightly but insisted on making the bodies as real as the photographs and pictures they had seen in the books in the book corner.

Each child chose a butterfly to stick onto card, which they then cut out. A ring was made from a length of card about 1cm wide to attach to the butterfly's underside, making a simple finger puppet. One or two of the older children only glued a strip of card to the abdomen of their butterfly so that when the finger ring was added to make their puppet, the wings could flap quite realistically when they moved their finger up and down quickly.

Rhythmical ribbons

The idea for this activity came when I was watching a couple of children in the garden, playing with a pink hoop. A child was swinging the hoop around his head while his friend jumped up and down trying to catch it. Suddenly a gust of wind caught the hoop, it dropped and spun on the ground. The boys leapt after it and continued with their game. It reminded me of rhythmic gymnastics.

Rhythmic gymnastics combines elements of ballet, theatrical dance, gymnastics and apparatus manipulation. The boys were handling the hoop with flexibility and were pivoting, spinning, leaping and balancing; only a short step away from rhythmical movement?

Rhythmic gymnastics is a sport for individuals, pairs or groups (usually five) where ropes, balls, hoops, clubs or ribbons are used for artistic effect while exercising to music. The exercises are designed to promote grace of movement, muscular flexibility and good posture, choreographed into a dance and tumble routine on the floor.

Obviously the type of exercises that can be tried with children may be limited by the equipment you have available within your setting. We used hoops, quoits and ribbons to highlight rhythm with the children. However, you can use squares of light fabric, scarves from your dressing-up box or strips of crepe paper for flowing and floating movements.

Use familiar music so that the children can be spontaneous with their actions. Keep the extracts short to maintain the children's interest and attention. If the music is new, give children the opportunity to listen to it before you start the activity, giving them a chance to 'feel' the music; suggest, as they sit listening, they sway or move their hands and feet to the rhythm.

Ideas with ribbon, paper streamer or scarf in one hand:

- With arm outstretched, swing the scarf in a large circular motion in various directions: over the head, out to the side or out in front of the body.
- Draw snakes in the air by shaking the outstretched arm.
- Make spirals with small, quick circles.
- Throw the scarf up in the air and catch it while moving to the music, perhaps twirl around before catching it again.
- Balance on one leg while twirling the scarf.
- Lie on the floor with arm stretched upwards and circle the scarf over the head or out to the side.

Experiment with different widths and lengths of ribbon or fabric. Can figures of eight or letters be drawn? What happens if the ribbon is attached to a piece of dowelling held in the hand? Why not try similar activities using hoops, quoits or beanbags related to your colour theme?

Section 9: Black and white

	KUW	CLL	PSRN	C	P	PSE
169 About black and white	•	•				
170 Strikingly striped	•			•	•	
171 Opposites attract	•	•		•		
172 Silhouette lotto		•	•			•
173 Outline lotto cards		•			•	
174 Silhouette lotto cards		•			•	
175 Shapes, shadows and symmetry	•	•	•	•	•	
176 Shapes, shadows and symmetry page		•				

About black and white

About black

Black is the ultimate dark shade of colours and makes lighter colours and photographs stand out. It can make these colours appear brighter. Teamed with orange, black suggests Hallowe'en to many children.

Black, like other colours, has positive and negative aspects in the way it can be perceived. It very often signifies death or mourning, sadness and fear, but can also imply sophistication, elegance and style, being visually slimming in clothing. It is associated with authority, especially in the uniforms of the police and guards: the men in black. A black tie 'do' is usually a very formal party occasion where the men wear black suits and ties and the women wear long black evening dresses. However, the 'black market', 'blackmail' and 'blacklisting' depict the less positive nature of the colour black. If you live in Australia and some areas of Britain, a black cat crossing your path will bring you good luck. In other places, a black cat is thought to bring misfortune.

Black does not reflect light, so black fabrics and paint were ideal to cover windows in war time as black-outs.

Black is used as an essential element in creating drama or mystery. It is the colour of night and can represent 'evil'. Our imagination is often stimulated by darkness, the lack of colour in black is very different from the realities of daylight.

About white

White is thought of as a sacred and pure colour, signifying cleanliness, innocence, simplicity and reverence. It is associated with hospitals, especially doctors, nurses and dentists. White is also thought of as the colour of winter and snow.

Like black, white blends well with almost any colour as it is seen as a neutral colour. However, too much bright white light can be blinding and cause headaches for some people.

Again, as with all the colours, there are positive and negative connotations to white. In most Western countries it is the colour of choice for brides; whereas in the East, white is the colour of mourning and funerals. A 'white knuckle ride' is fast and can be exciting or very frightening. A 'white elephant' could be a rare and valuable item or something unwanted and discarded.

However, in a number of cultures black and white are both the traditional funeral colours. Black is for the loss and mourning of the person who has died whereas white is for their passing into the heavens.

I have always enjoyed thinking about and designing displays and, though some work out better than others, my favourites often include colours. Black and white together creates very striking, eye-catching, clear and vibrant results.

One of the first displays I ever produced with the children in my group concerned T*he Rabbits' Wedding* by the illustrator and author Garth Williams. The story is about a black rabbit marrying a white rabbit. However, the book was banned in America in the late 1950s due to its supposed theme of interracial love. Garth Williams was of the opinion that animals with white or black fur are not considered blood relations to human beings, that the two rabbits just looked picturesque together and the story had no hidden message regarding different races. The children had no idea of the controversy surrounding the story, they just enjoyed painting two-foot-high rabbits, one black, one white, with a moonlit black sky and white trees in the background. It was very simple but extremely striking visually.

When the giant panda Ching-Ching died in London Zoo in 1985, our school began a theme on endangered animals. The nursery was allocated a table and wall display in the hall and the children wanted to do 'Ching-Ching. We had a pale green background with a three-and-a-half-foot high collage and painted Ching-Ching sitting in front of bamboo canes and leaves painted by the children on the background. After chatting with the children about the table display, they decided to make clay Giant Pandas which they painted black and white. Some of the clay models were only about three centimetres in height, others were almost ten centimetres and most looked like bears! Another striking black and white display.

But one of my all-time favourites was when we were talking with the children about road safety. The majority of children walked to school and were aware of looking both ways and listening before crossing the roads. As they got nearer school the 'lollipop lady' would help them cross safely. Some children used a pedestrian crossing with traffic lights, understanding the red man meant WAIT as the button was pressed and only to cross when the green man appeared. These children all lived the other side of the zebra crossing and desperately wanted to cross it – in case they saw a zebra crossing!

How could I resist that display? The thought still makes me smile. Kitchen roll tubes painted in rings of black and white, round orange balloons attached to the top as Belisha beacons, on either side of a painted zebra crossing with . . . a zebra crossing it, strikingly striped!

Opposites attract

Before computers and the Internet were commonplace in schools, a topic would often begin with a browse through books, magazines and files of photos and cards (collected over the years for this purpose) for appropriate pictures.

On this particular occasion, we were looking for something to spark off an idea when a child picked out a postcard of an Australian black swan. What had caught the child's eye were the light-grey cygnets next to their mother. He wondered why they were not black like their mum. I explained that birds often take up to a year or more for their plumage to resemble their parents'. He looked very closely at the picture and noticed some white feathers on the adult's back. They were, in fact, the bird's flight feathers but there was no photograph of a black swan flying so that its wings could be seen. 'Will this penguin do instead then?' he said. We understood his logic when he produced a picture of a penguin showing its black wings and white underbelly, the opposite of the black swan – our new theme was born!

By the end of the week we had black and white pictures, postcards, photographs and books depicting animals, birds, insects, fish and even a whale; all were black and white. Soft toys were brought in: black and white ring-tailed lemurs, a polar bear with its black nose, penguins and badgers. Plastic zoo and farm animals including a cow and a sheepdog, a zebra and a racoon, added to the display too. We were surprised by the number and array of black and white animals that the children had.

We came to the conclusion that black and white together is often very conspicuous and eye-catching.

A parent brought in a framed swallowtail butterfly that an uncle had given him. We used a magnifying glass to look more closely at the wings. Some children drew remarkable 'copies' of the butterfly with pencils and black crayons on bright white paper, and the stark contrast of light and dark drew your attention straight away.

As the theme grew, we realised just how many birds are black and white that are resident in Britain. It would have saved a great deal of time if we had had computers and the Internet to help in our search. However, the excitement the children had on discovering another white and black animal in a book was something I'm glad I witnessed.

Silhouette lotto

This game was devised originally for a little boy in my class in a special school in the 1970s. He had cerebral palsy and was learning to communicate using Bliss symbols, eye contact and a head pointer.

Two or three of the other children showed an interest in Peter's symbols, some of which were pictorial in nature. I thought that a game using some of the picture-type symbols would give the children a greater understanding of other forms of communication while reinforcing and practising the skills Peter needed to communicate with others. I also wanted the whole experience to be a game for Peter and the other children, not extra 'work'.

The four boards on the following black and white lotto game pages can be used in a variety of ways, although I'm sure no explanation is needed on how to play lotto; i.e. bingo with pictures!

The activity can be used by a single child just as easily as playing the game with a small group. However, before the game can begin, both pages need photocopying twice onto card. One set of pages will be the boards, one set need to be cut into separate pictures to be used for matching in the game.

How to play the game

Each child has a board. All the single cards are shuffled and placed face downwards in a pile. The children take turns to take a card and check as to whether or not it matches a picture on their board.

- Use the silhouette (black) pictures to match with the black picture boards and the outline (white) pictures to match to the outline (white) picture boards.
  or
- Use the black pictures to match with the white picture boards and vice versa.

Ordinary lotto

The white (outline) pictures can also be used as a regular lotto game without using the silhouette images or boards. Colour in each outline picture to match the colours you have chosen for the boards. (This does not necessarily have to be done by the early years' practitioner.)

Children like to decide on the colours needed for each picture. Suggest each child works together in a pair to make the board and cards match. This will encourage co-operation and sharing, concentration and perseverance, respect for one another's ideas and develops communication skills, as well as being a very social occasion.

The pictures have been chosen because many are of no specific colour and can be used to complement whatever your theme is. Mix and match by adding the pictures from the 'Games page' in Section 1: Activities for all, to make new boards and playing cards.

Outline lotto cards page

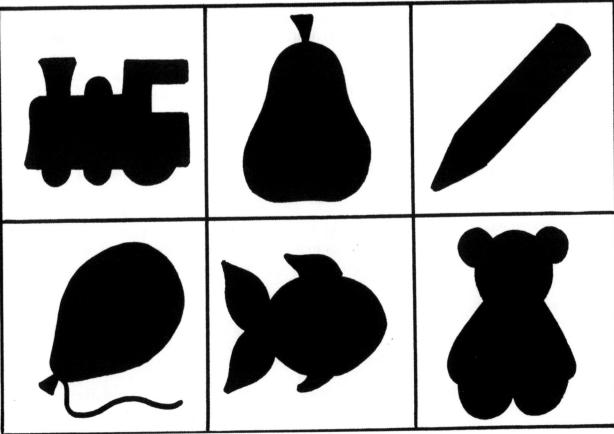

Shapes

These two activities evolved after I had watched a two-year-old using a pair of scissors. He had been sitting next to a couple of very capable four-year-olds who had drawn pictures, cut them out and stuck them on to paper. He asked to do the same, took a butterfly picture from the table and began cutting. He was completely engrossed in snipping away at the sugar paper with the butterfly drawn on it. When he had finished cutting and put down the scissors, he burst into tears.

On the table in front of him were several scraps of paper, but no butterfly! So, like a puzzle, we put the butterfly back together, well almost. He stuck each piece onto a sheet of paper like the girls until most of the outline could be seen again. He was happy to take it home as the first picture he had successfully cut out.

It started me thinking about activities that a child could manage with very little cutting ability with an end result that would be unique and creative. All that was required was black and white sugar paper, scissors and glue.

Either start with an outline already cut out on black paper or the children can make their own. The example Christine and I have used on the 'Shapes, shadows and symmetry page' is a fish. Because of its flowing lines and plain design, it is fairly easy to copy, but most simple outlines will work just as well.

Initially ask each child to make just three or four cuts across the outline. Then they place the pieces on to a contrasting sheet of white paper, with small gaps in between each piece. If they are happy with the result, the pieces can be stuck down. Obviously more cuts can be made but the fitting together of the pieces will be more difficult. Each picture will be unique and, although the end results may look similar, they will all be different.

Shadows and symmetry

Manipulating the blades of scissors is a difficult procedure, so this activity only requires the ability to tear paper.

Put the straight edges of a sheet of black paper and white paper on top of each other. Tear shapes into this edge. Then lay the torn edges together with the black sheet above the white sheet. Place the torn white pieces in the black paper gaps and vice versa, making shadows on the white paper.

TIP

Use paper clips or staples to hold the sheets together while tearing to ensure the tears are the same in black as in white.

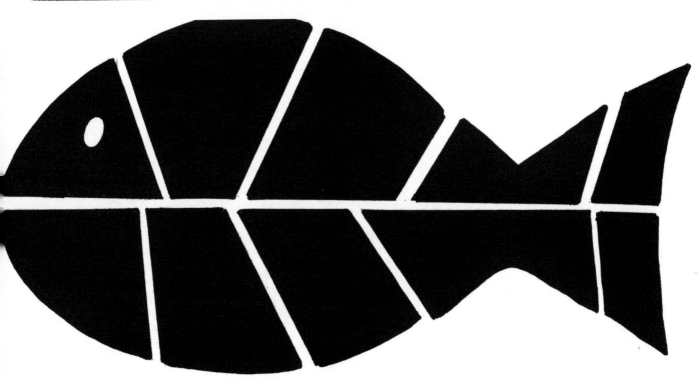

Section 10: Silver and gold

	KUW	CLL	PSRN	C	P	PSE
177 About gold and silver	•	•				•
178 Mining for gold	•	•				•
179 1st, 2nd, 3rd		•	•			•
180 Cattle grid game					•	
181 Panning for gold	•	•			•	•
182 Silver goldfish	•	•	•	•	•	•
183 Goldfish differences activity page	•	•				
184 Mine a metal	•		•	•	•	•
185 Mine a metal maze page		•			•	

About gold

Gold shares many attributes with the colour yellow. It is a warm colour that can be bright and cheerful, as well as traditional and sombre.

Gold is a precious metal and therefore the colour gold is associated with wealth, extravagance and prosperity and is the traditional gift given to celebrate a fiftieth wedding anniversary. Gold often represents the colour of the heavens and is used to decorate statues of Buddha and religious temples, especially in Egyptian pharaoh burial chambers.

As with all colours, gold suggests both positive and negative qualities. The saying 'All that glitters is not gold' suggests that appearances can be deceptive. A person who is a 'gold digger' pretends friendship or interest in a person just to gain their money, whereas a person who is 'solid gold' is outstanding or the best of the best. A 'golden boy' is a favoured person, and a 'gold star' suggests praise and commendation.

Fields of ripening corn, wheat or rice are often referred to as fields of gold because of the overall colour in the sun. However, the Golden Gate Bridge in San Francisco is not named after its colour (which is reddy-orange), but after the strait that it spans.

About silver

Silver is a cool colour without the warmth of gold. It is a precious metal and often symbolises richness. Silver is the traditional twenty-fifth wedding anniversary gift.

It can be glamorous and distinguished, sleek and elegant. To be described as 'silver-haired' suggests that the person is ageing gracefully as opposed to 'grey-haired' people who are often seen as merely old.

As with gold, there are contradictory sayings associated with silver. A person who is 'silver-tongued' can speak eloquently and is often witty while doing so, yet a 'silver-tongued devil' who speaks articulately, is often lying or insincere in what they say. A derisory comment aimed at a person born into a wealthy family and who has no need to work for a living is 'born with a silver spoon in their mouth'. 'Every cloud has a silver lining' suggests that misfortune has its consolations.

A silverback gorilla is a mature adult male gorilla, usually more than twelve years old. Until they develop the distinctive patch of silver hair on their back, they are called blackback gorillas.

Discuss why an eagle or retriever dog might be called golden and a fox or fish, silver. What about goldfish and goldfinches? What type of service or screen is silver? Is silence golden? How fine is silver sand?

Aiming for gold

Are we aiming for gold or will silver do?

A great number of sports days at school promote the idea that no one wins, it's all about taking part. We've often heard the phrase. Do we or the children really believe it? Even at an early age, children understand that if nobody loses, nobody wins, and to receive a prize for trying their best is an empty gesture.

In the 1950s when I was at school, we had winners and losers. I knew I was a loser at running an ordinary race, I just wasn't fast enough. I stood a better chance in the sack, egg and spoon or, even better, the three-legged race, where balance and co-ordination are required to a greater extent than speed.

Even though I rarely won, I remember our sports days as fun. Our headmaster always thanked everyone for attending the races, cheering and shouting was a must for everyone watching, including our mums (dads were rarely at these sort of events). Clapping all the contenders at the end of each race was compulsory and everyone received a sweet for their hard work in running. However, there was always a winner, someone in second place and a third runner-up. They all received a certificate or ribbon and a house point and, of course, the sweet!

How would you feel if no one could catch you in the playground when playing 'tig' but your energy was not rewarded on sports day because there are no winners? You know you came first, everyone saw you cross the line first, what is so wrong in being a winner?

The competitive ethos in any sport is to do your very best to win.

Imagine watching your local football team kicking the ball to anyone on the pitch, scoring goals at either end and just having fun? Where would athletes be if they pushed their bodies to the peak of physical fitness, training for months, to be the first to cross the line just to be told 'Thanks for taking part'?

There will always be winners and losers in every aspect of life, not just when it comes to sports days, and they can be a valuable tool in understanding our strengths and weaknesses, to accept or improve our performance but to always try to do our best. If competition is supposed to threaten the emotional well-being of a child, why are there school league tables and SATs?

Children usually know whether they are good enough to try to win and, without sportsmen and women going for gold, there would be very little point in training for the ultimate Olympic Games or even the Grand National.

1st, 2nd or 3rd?

Following on from the previous page is a game which we often played so that children could begin to understand about ordinal numbers.

Ordinal numbers are the words representing objects placed in order to signify the object's position, i.e. first, second, twentieth or last. The use of ordinal numbers can relate to chronology, size, instructions, priorities or importance, etc. Ordinal numbers are probably most familiar when used to describe positions in a race or league table.

The idea of the game is to be the first cow through the gate to be milked, followed by a second, then a third, and so on.

Ingredients
A photocopy of the 'Cattle grid game', preferably onto card, small world cows, an old spare dice, sticky labels (large enough to cover sides of dice), scissors, and gold, silver and coloured self-adhesive stars.

Method
1. Stick labels on the sides of the dice to cover the numbers 3, 4, 5 and 6.
2. Draw one or two dots or numerals 1 and 2 on the labels to make three sides showing 1 and three sides 2.

To play the game
1. Each child chooses a cow from the farm animals and places it in a rectangle at the edge of the field opposite the open gate. Only one cow is allowed in each space.
2. To move nearer the gate, the dice is thrown by each child in turn and the cow is moved according to the number shown on the dice.
3. The cows can only move forwards or sideways, not diagonally. For example, if a 2 is thrown, the cow can move two spaces forwards, two spaces sideways or one forwards and one sideways (making two moves)
4. Sometimes the cows have to move backwards as they get closer to the gate so that there is never more than one cow in each space.
5. The first through the gate for milking is awarded the gold star, the second wins silver, the third bronze or whichever colour you have decided to award.
6. Every cow who gets through the gate for milking is awarded a star, so everyone who finishes the game wins!

Alternatives
- Stickers with 1st, 2nd, 3rd, 4th, 5th, etc. written on them can be awarded to players who successfully get their cow to the milking shed.
- Small world sheep can be used to get ready for shearing. This game can be used alongside the 'Baa Baa Black Sheep' theme in *Activities for Individual Learning Through Rhyme*, published by Continuum, 2010.
- Play the game outdoors by drawing a grid with chalks and throw a beanbag into a square to move forwards.

Cattle grid game

PART 2
COLOUR

Section 10
**Silver
and gold**

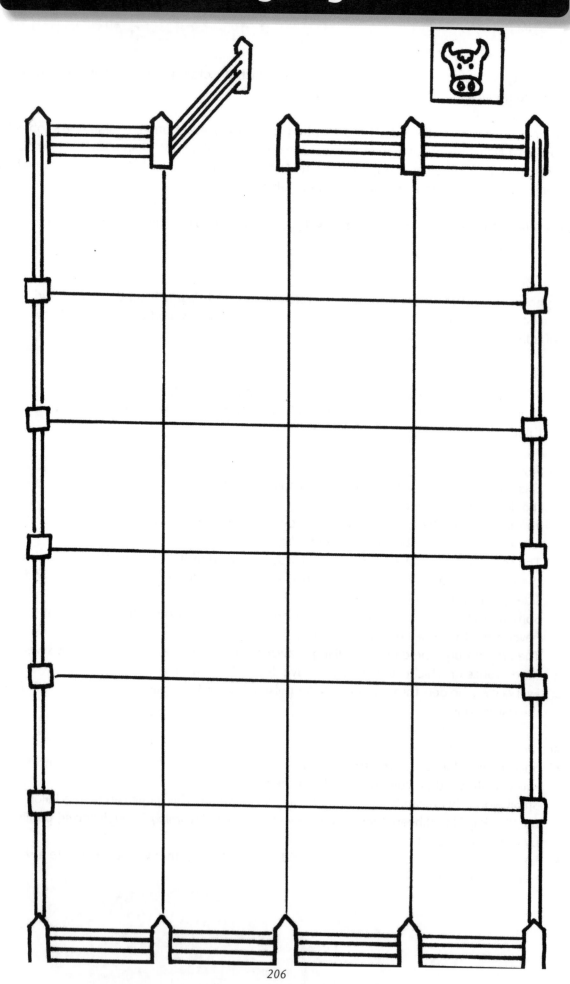

The great Gold Rush happened in America when gold was discovered near San Francisco in California in the 1840s. Thousands of people (prospectors) trekked across America in the hope of making their fortune. The gold was found in the gravel and sand of the rivers. Many inexperienced prospectors often mistook shiny yellow pyrite chunks for golden nuggets and this gave rise to the term 'Fools' Gold'.

The technique of gold panning involves a lot of patience and skill, but is easy to pick up after the first few attempts, although not everyone is lucky enough to come away with flakes of gold, while nuggets are extremely rare.

When gold panning, gravel from the banks of a river where the sediment is finest is placed into the pan, until about half full. Then the pan is filled with the river water and gently swirled. As gold is much denser than rock, it should settle in the bottom of the pan, while all other sediment separates to the sides.

Finding gold

Some theme parks give children the opportunity to pan for gold and, with a bit of 'tweaking', your sand or water trays can be used to go gold panning in your setting.

Ingredients
Wet sand in a tray or container, water and container, measuring cup, waterproof aprons, gold pony beads or small pieces of gravel (painted gold), shallow dishes or trays

Method
1. Add some of the beads or painted gravel to the wet sand and mix well so that they cannot be seen.
2. Waterproof aprons should be worn at all times.

> **TIP**
> Explain that gold prospectors were not always successful in finding gold. Several attempts using small amounts of sand may be required to find one piece of 'gold'.

3. The child puts a measure of wet sand into their shallow dish and pours water on top.
4. The 'pan' is gently swirled around so that the water starts to separate the sand and the 'gold' can be seen.

> **TIP**
> Close supervision will be needed for younger or less able children who are still developing their control, balance and co-ordination skills.

5. Once a piece of gold is found, the child pours the excess water back into the water container and tips the wet sand back into the sand tray.

Panning for gold

> **TIP**
>
> If you have a 'gold rush' to participate in this activity, decide on the maximum number of 'finds' before another child can take their turn at prospecting.

Although silver is mined differently, there is no reason why the 'gold' cannot be exchanged for silver or added into the mix too!

Silver goldfish

At one pre-school I visited, they had a plastic tank with three goldfish in it. Each was different; one had a double tail, another had a growth like a raspberry on its head and the third was black, white, orange and brown in colour. Not one was gold but the fish with the double tail definitely had scales that looked silvery in the light.

That observation was how our 'Goldfish differences activity page' came about. The children told me about their goldfish; about the many types, that most are not gold at all and there are goldfish that have a silver appearance too! Goldfish are a member of the carp family and vary in body shape as well as size and colour. Some have no dorsal fin, others have two tails, but all are small ornamental freshwater fish that are often very hardy pets.

If your setting has no access to a fish pond or an aquarium, images can easily be found on the Internet or by browsing through books from the library to enable children to observe closely the types of goldfish.

The 'Goldfish differences activity page' can be used in several ways to enhance other areas of the foundation stage.

Knowledge and understanding of the world will be encouraged, not least for finding the differences between each fish; by adding anything missing or altering the images to make them look the same, etc.

Fine motor skills can be enhanced by photocopying the activity page onto card and each fish being cut out by a child; make one fish a template for drawing around, the other a threading card with holes punched around its edge. Tracing cards are another alternative activity for developing hand–eye co-ordination.

Enlarge or reduce the size of the goldfish when photocopying and use collage materials, crayons or paints, to make an aquarium, thus promoting creativity. Give the children the opportunity to draw or paint their own fish and use them all to decorate a box with an open side to resemble a fish tank, perhaps with gravel in the bottom. Invite the children to design an aquarium to increase their skills in problem-solving and reasoning.

Play the flapping fish game to promote personal, social and emotional development. Each child makes a fish shaped from silver foil and places it on the floor. Then flap a rolled-up newspaper near to the fish to make it move, see whose fish flies farthest.

The story of *The Rainbow Fish* by Marcus Pfister can accompany all these activities and will encourage children to listen and observe as well as promoting understanding and communication skills.

Goldfish differences activity page

Although gold can be found in rivers and streams, even in Britain, it is also mined underground like silver. Silver occurs in a native form but is more usually combined with other metals as an ore that needs to be washed and smelted to produce the metal. Silver is often found with lead ore.

Hard rock mining is done below ground where the ore is encased in rock. Some mines are over 3,000 metres deep. The ore is brought to the surface through tunnels and shafts. Dynamite is used to open up the rock walls to loosen the ore, hammers and chisels remove smaller pieces of metal and the spades are to shovel the debris into carts which are wheeled along to the shafts to be shifted.

Our 'Mine a metal maze' is designed so that whichever entrance to the mine is chosen, the child will find gold, silver or mining implements. The maze can be altered with the use of correction fluid or tape to 'erase' some of the lines. This will open up the mine fully to make access to all areas much easier.

To encourage a child's thinking and reasoning skills, block one or two of the entrances so that the child has to work out which lines need to be 'erased' to reach the depths of the mine, the metal, pick-axe, spade or dynamite.

One play corner we devised was to use our wooden climbing frame as a mine. We covered the outside of the frame with corrugated card and placed the wooden slats inside at different levels to suggest the mine shaft. The inside was covered with black sugar paper, with scraps of silver foil attached with glue from a glue stick (for easy removal). Silver beads were 'hidden' on the floor of the mine under pieces of scrap paper, representing the debris and stones from the walls of the mine. The children climbed up the ladder to enter and exit the mine shaft. The mine was a very popular imaginative play activity which led on to a pirate-based theme. I think some children thought they were finding buried treasure left by pirates in the mine!

We had to replenish the silver regularly, as the children then used the foil pieces in various ways. Some made shiny collages, adding sequins and sweet-wrappers to their pictures. Some of the card foil pieces were stuck back to back with a silver thread in between and strung together to make mobiles which hung from the tree outside. When the wind blew, the mobiles spun around, caught the light from the sun and made glittery patterns over the playground.

Mine a metal maze

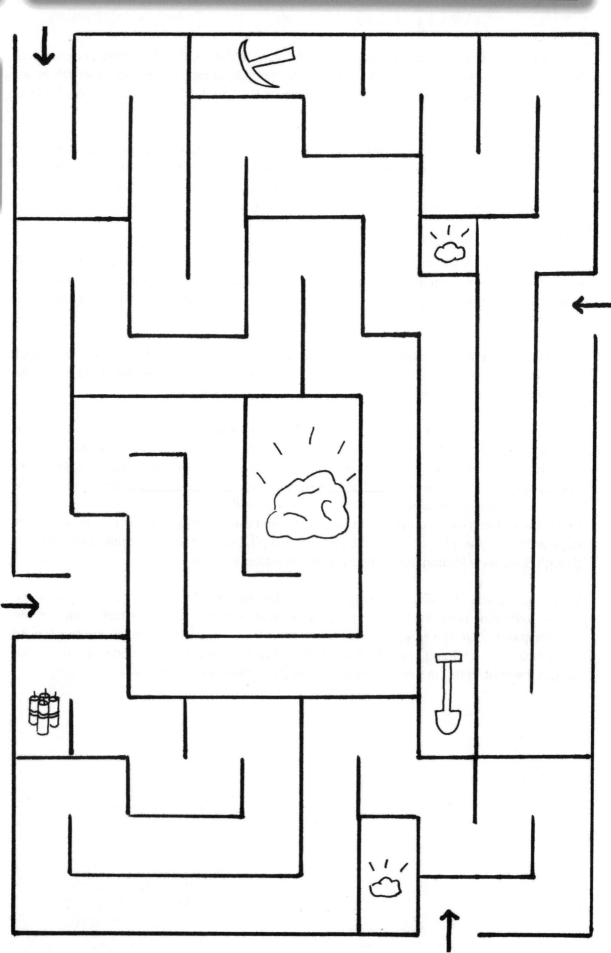